BE BLESSED

Words and Music by JAMES HARRIS III,
TERRY LEWIS, JAMES WRIGHT
and YOLANDA ADAMS

Moderately slow, in 2

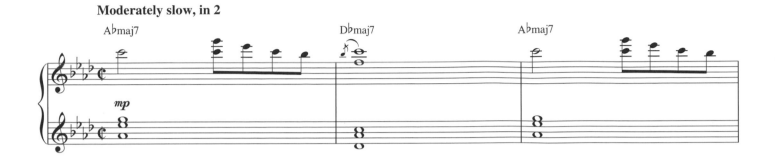

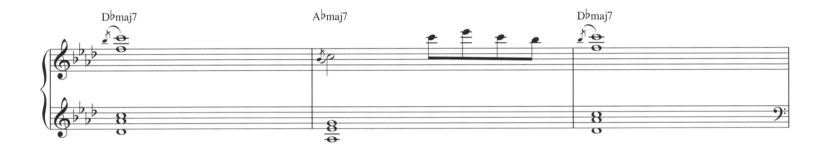

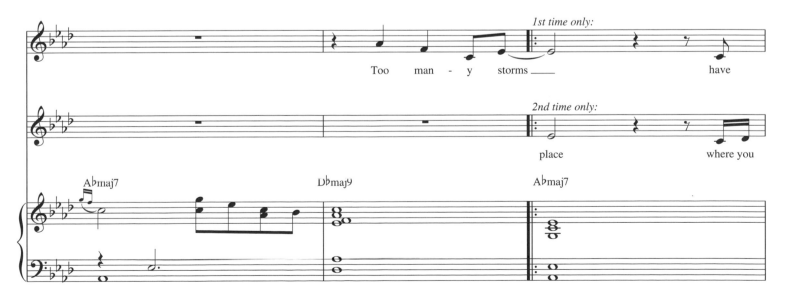

Too man-y storms ____ have

1st time only:

place

2nd time only:

where you

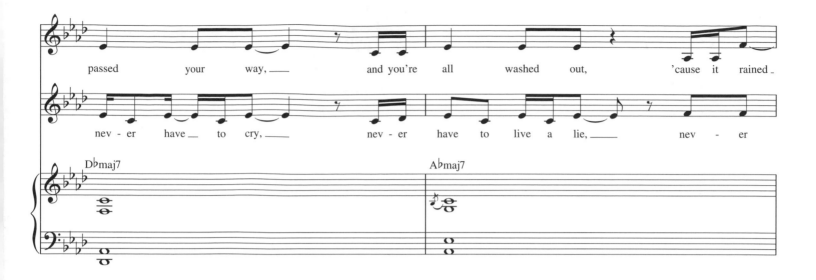

passed your way, ____ and you're all washed out, 'cause it rained _

nev - er have __ to cry, ____ nev - er have to live a lie, ____ nev - er

D♭maj7   A♭maj7

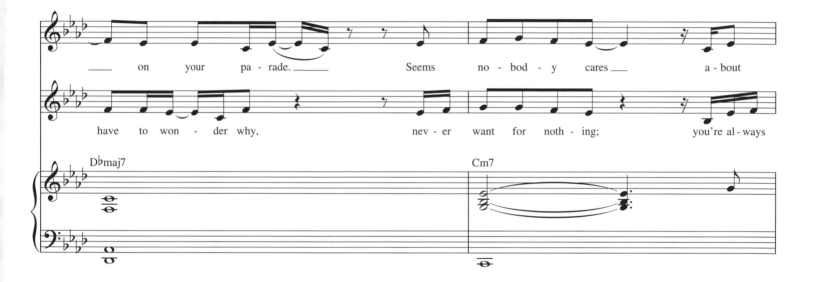

____ on your pa - rade. ____ Seems no - bod - y cares ____ a - bout

have to won - der why, nev - er want for noth - ing; you're al - ways

D♭maj7   Cm7

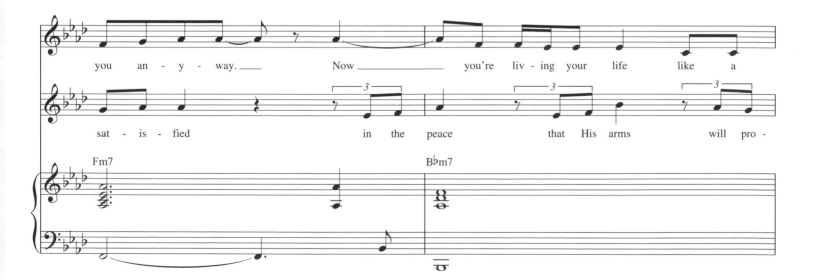

you an - y - way. ____ Now _____ you're liv - ing your life like a

sat - is - fied in the peace that His arms will pro -

Fm7   B♭m7

cast - a - way. _____ Search _____ for strength in - side; _____ was it

vide. _____ He will _____ e - rase _____ an - y

Eb9sus   Abmaj7

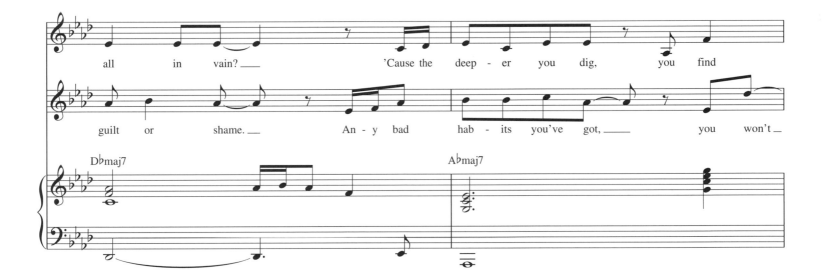

all in vain? _____ 'Cause the deep - er you dig, you find

guilt or shame. _____ An - y bad hab - its you've got, _____ you won't _____

Dbmaj7   Abmaj7

more and more pain. _____ Don't let your _____ to - mor - row be like

_____ wan - na do 'em a - gain. Yes, we all can change; I _____

Dbmaj9   Cm7

8

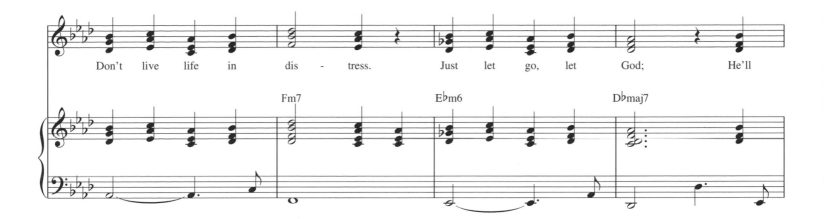

Don't live life in dis - tress. Just let go, let God; He'll

Fm7   Ebm6   Dbmaj7

work it out for _____ you.

Fm7   Bbm7   Db/Eb

I pray that your soul will be blessed for -

Bbm/Ab   Ab   Fm7

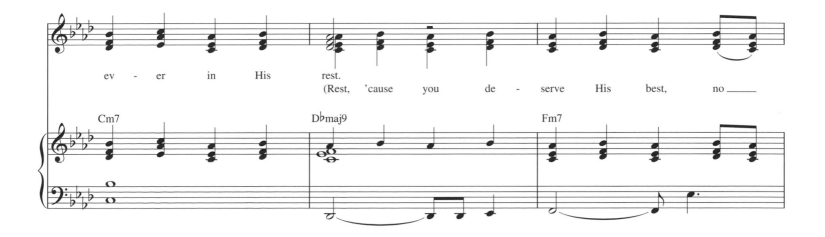

ev - er in His rest.
(Rest, 'cause you de - serve His best, no _____

Cm7   Dbmaj9   Fm7

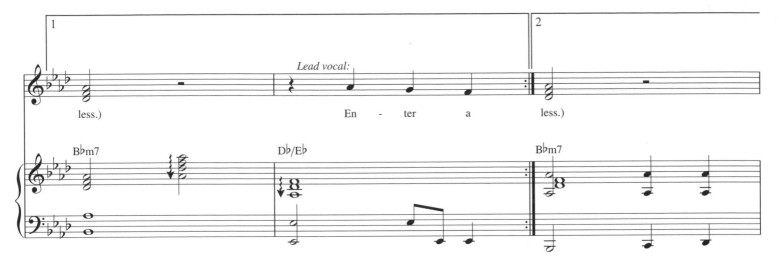

10

call - ing. _____ He'll keep you from fall - ing. _____

Cm7   D♭maj9   Cm7

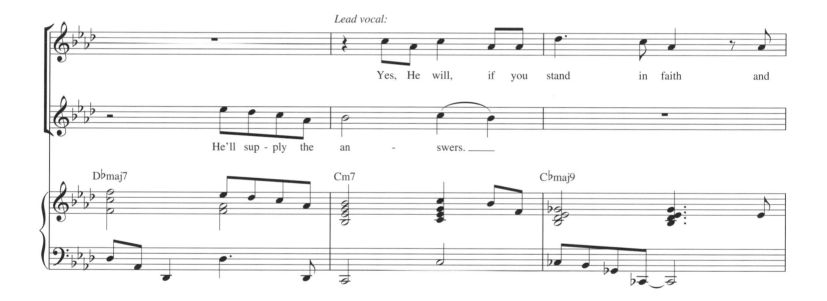

Lead vocal:

Yes, He will, if you stand in faith and

He'll sup - ply the an - swers. _____

D♭maj7   Cm7   C♭maj9

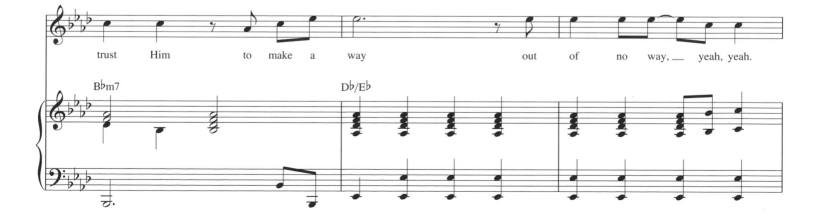

trust Him to make a way out of no way, _____ yeah, yeah.

B♭m7   D♭/E♭

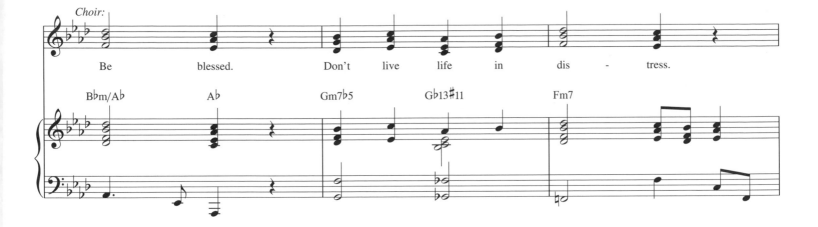

You've been through so much. Be blessed, __ from the bot - tom of

(less.)

your feet to the crown of your head. Your life be blessed,

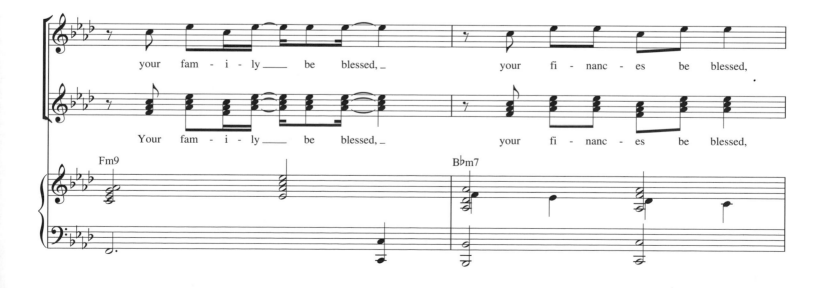

your fam - i - ly __ be blessed, __ your fi - nanc - es be blessed,

Your fam - i - ly __ be blessed, __ your fi - nanc - es be blessed,

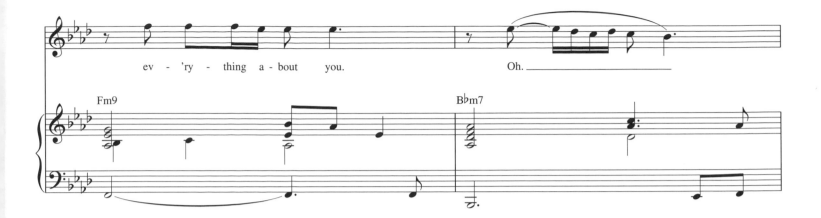

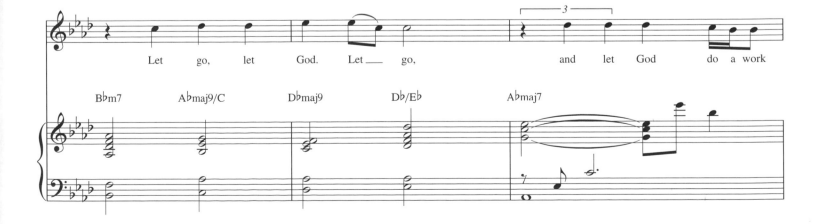

14

Additional Lyrics

Be blessed. Oh, be blessed.

Whatever you're going through,
Just know I'm praying for you.

Be blessed. Oh, be blessed.

He can change your situation in a minute.
Just be blessed.

Don't do anything that God would not have you to do.
Be blessed.

I know it ain't what you want right now, but it sure could be a lot worse.
Just be blessed.

Let Him do a work in you.
Hey, be blessed.

BLESSING IN THE STORM

Words and Music by
KIRK FRANKLIN

Recorded a half step higher.

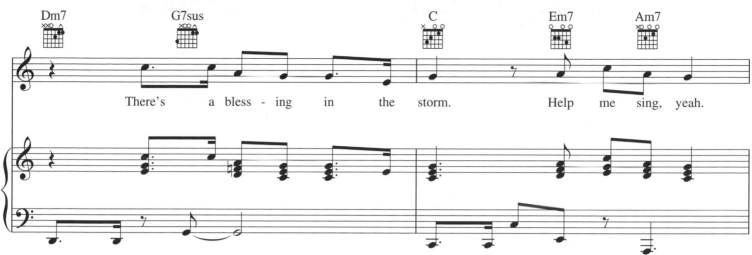

There's a bless - ing in the storm. Help me sing, yeah.

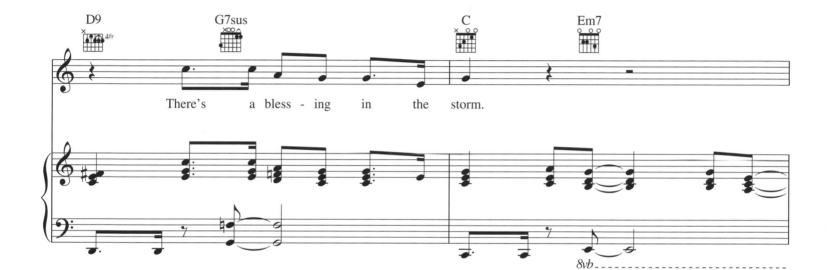

There's a bless - ing in the storm.

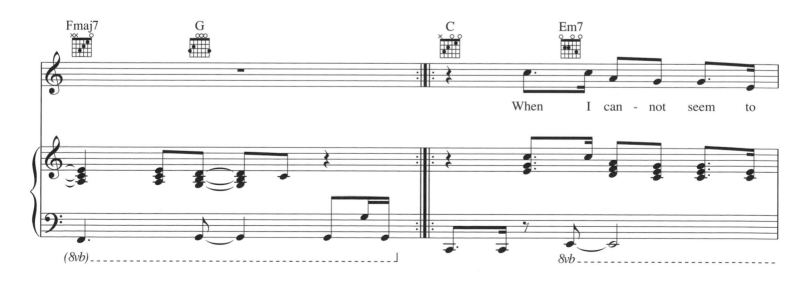

When I can - not seem to

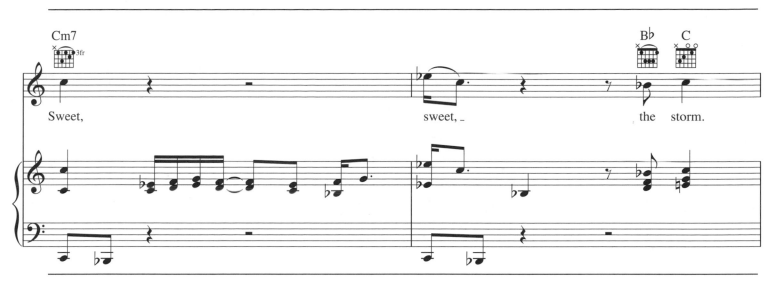

Sweet,   sweet, _   the storm.

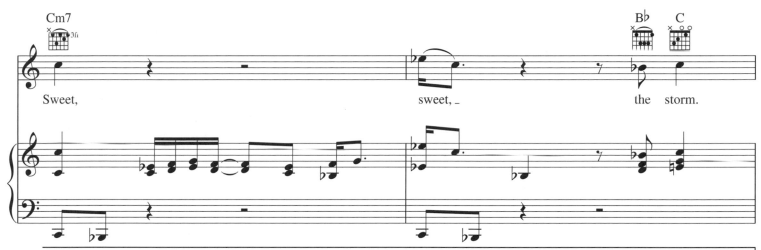

Sweet,   sweet, _   the storm.

Sweet,   sweet, _   the storm.

there's   a   bless - ing   in   the   storm.   Help   me   sing,   yeah,

there's a bless-ing in _____ the

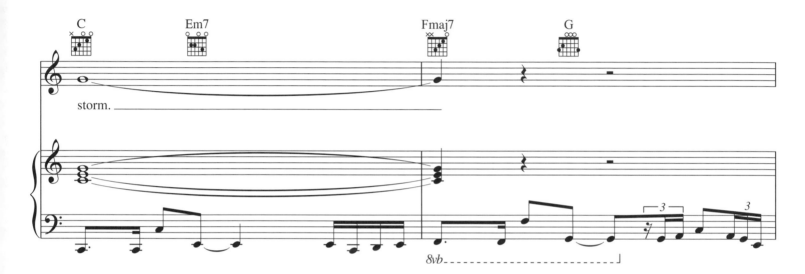

storm. _____

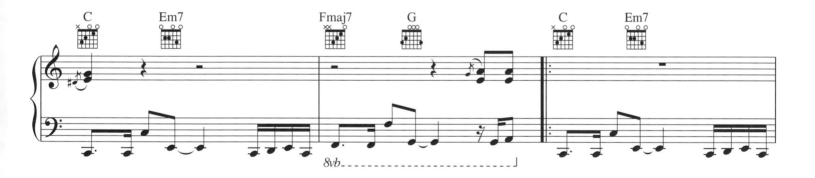

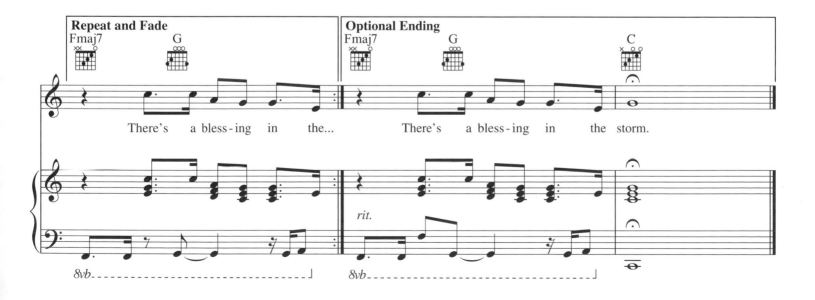

Repeat and Fade
There's a bless-ing in the...

Optional Ending
There's a bless-ing in the storm.

rit.

BELIEVER

Words and Music by ERICA ATKINS-CAMPBELL,
TRECINA ATKINS-CAMPBELL
and WARRYN CAMPBELL

* *Recorded a half step higher.*

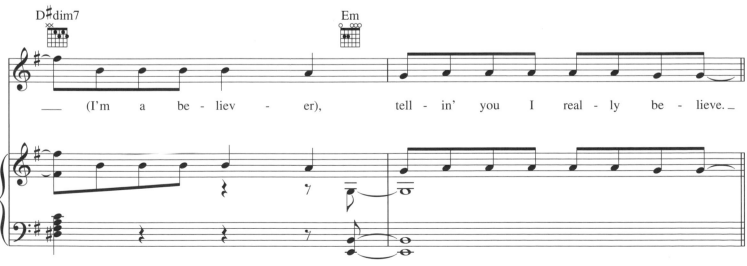

THE BEST IN ME

Words and Music by MARVIN SAPP
and AARON W. LINDSEY

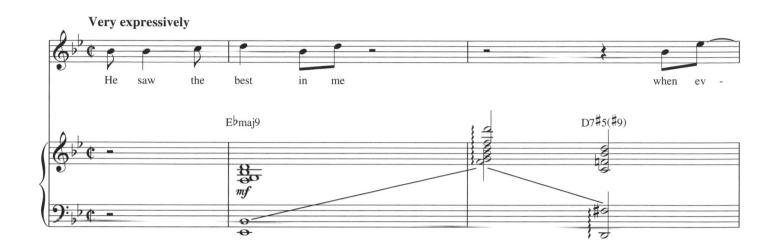

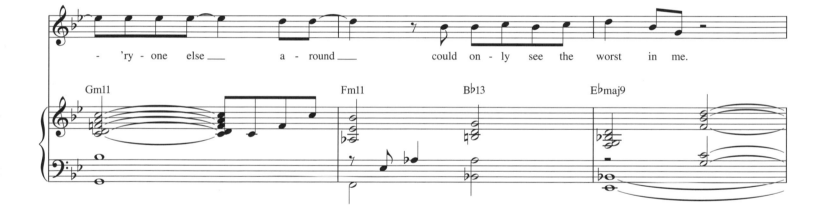

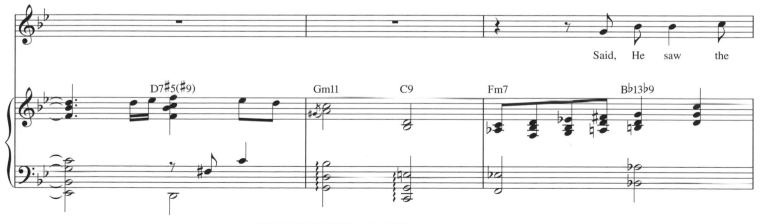

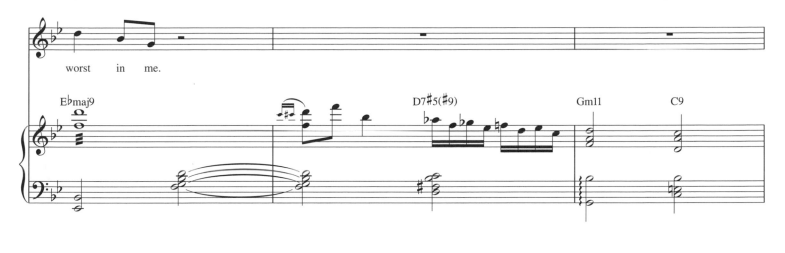

worst in me.

E♭maj9   D7♯5(♯9)   Gm11   C9

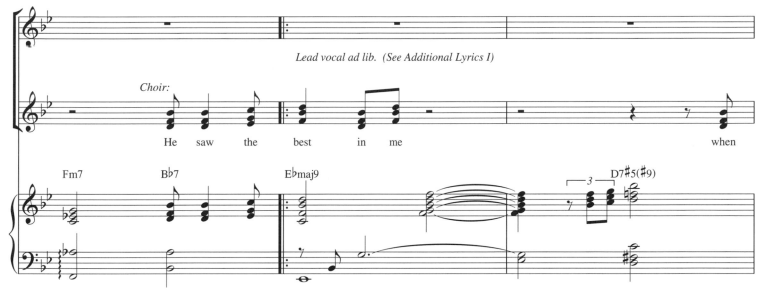

Lead vocal ad lib. (See Additional Lyrics I)

Choir:

He saw the best in me   when

Fm7   B♭7   E♭maj9   D7♯5(♯9)

ev - 'ry - one else___ a - round___ could on - ly see the worst in me.

Gm11   Fm7   B♭13   E♭maj7

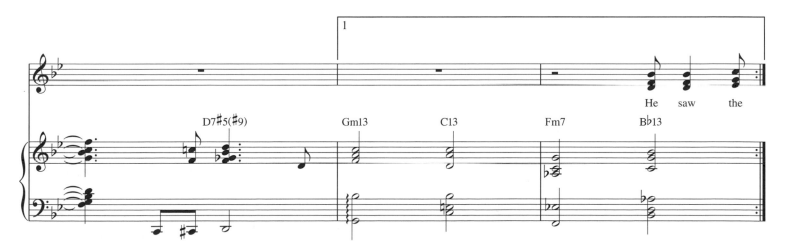

He saw the

D7♯5(♯9)   Gm13   C13   Fm7   B♭13

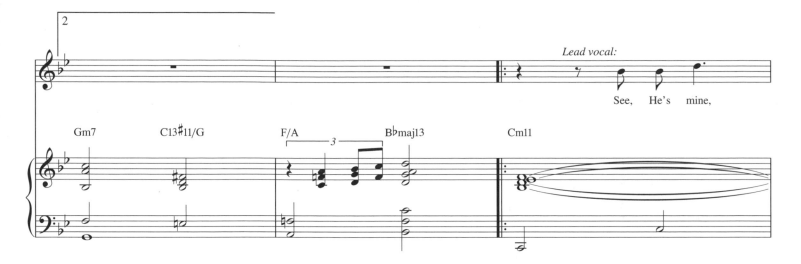

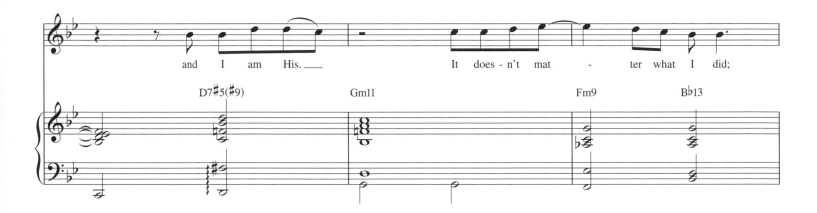

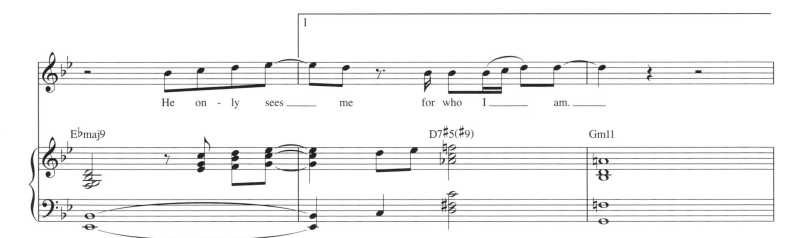

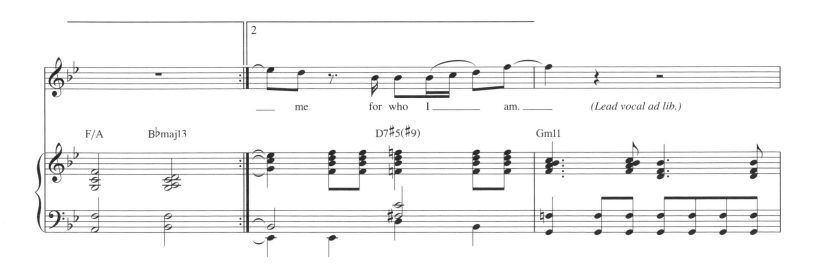

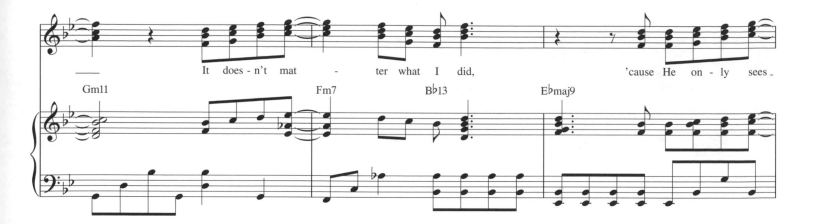

It does-n't mat - ter what I did, 'cause He on-ly sees

me for who I am.

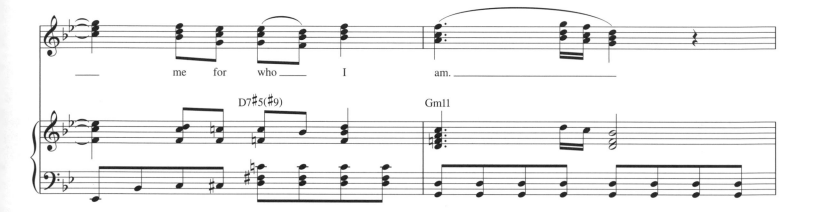

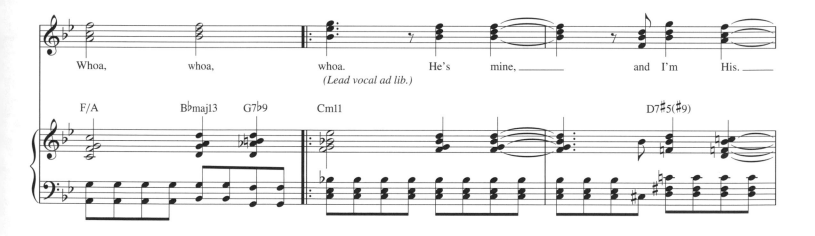

Whoa, whoa, whoa. He's mine, and I'm His.

(Lead vocal ad lib.)

It does-n't mat - ter what I did, 'cause He on-ly sees

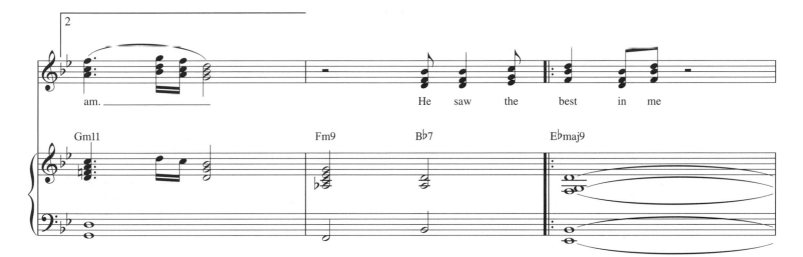

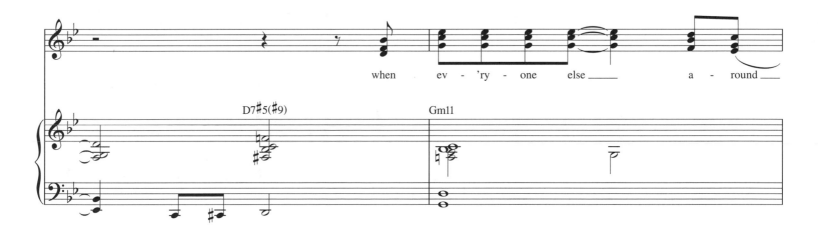

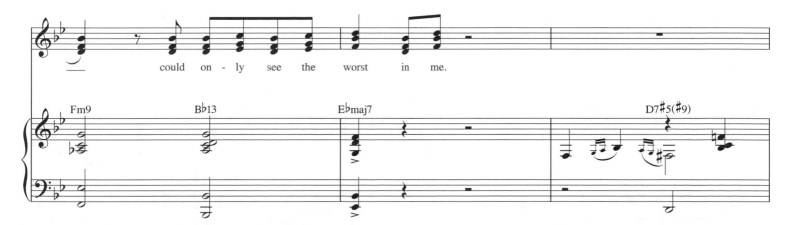

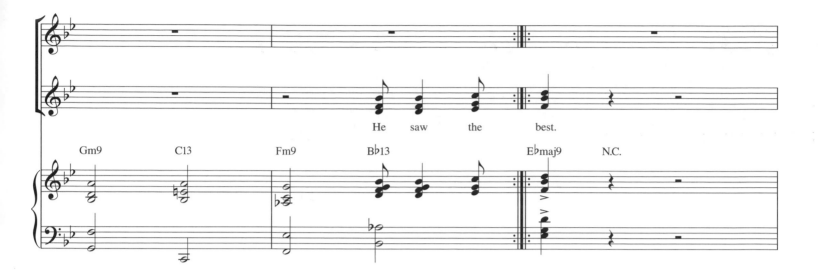

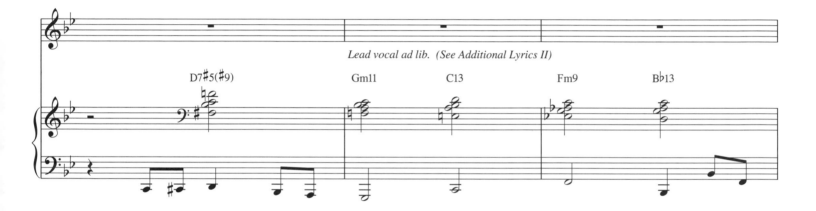

Lead vocal ad lib. (See Additional Lyrics II)

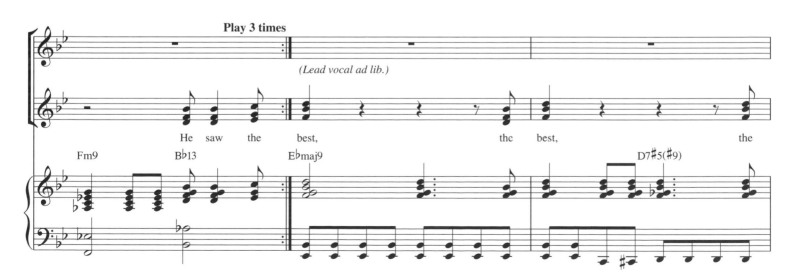

best, the best, the best, the

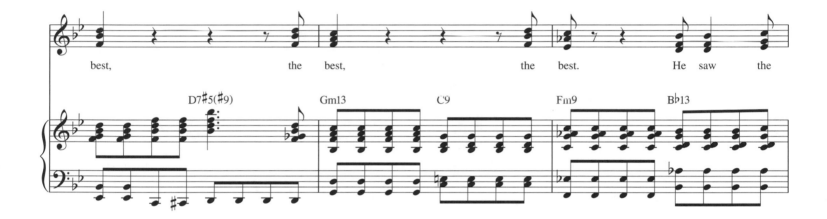

best, the best, the best. He saw the

best in me.

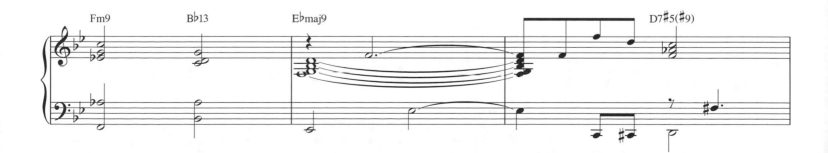

Additional Lyrics I

...When ev'ryone else around me
Could only see...
Does anybody have that testimony? When folk wrote you off,
Said you would never make it, what did He see?

Additional Lyrics II

(He saw the best)

I can't get no help up in here, because there are some folk in here that people have wrote you off,
Said you would never amount to anything, said that you would never end up being anywhere.
But Myron, tell them one more time, what did He see?

(He saw the best)

When Mama said you would never be nothing, when aunties and uncles said that you would never amount to anything,
When Daddy didn't come home anymore, He didn't look at you and say that you weren't gonna make it.
God looked at you, and what did He see?

(He saw the best)

Yeah, yeah, is there anybody in here tonight that's so very thankful that
God did not write you off, that He did not throw you away, that He picked you up?
He saw...

FAITHFUL TO BELIEVE

Words and Music by BYRON CAGE,
AARON LINDSEY and ADRIAN LINDSEY

Moderately, in 2

(Spoken:) Now unto Him...   that is able to do...   exceeding,

abundantly,   above what we could ask Him, or think...   ...Listen: Is there

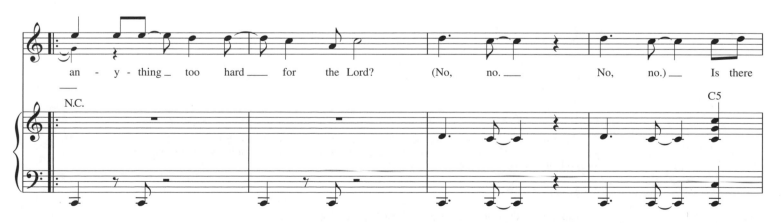

an-y-thing__ too hard__ for the Lord? (No, no.__ No, no.)__ Is there

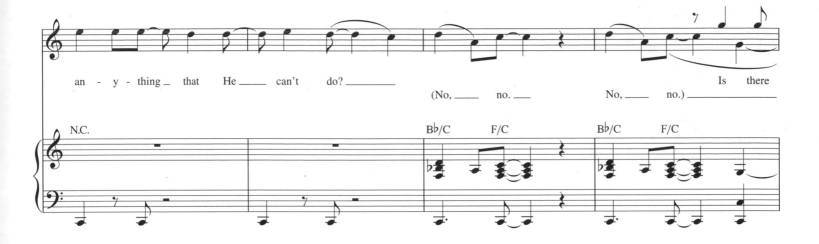

an-y-thing that He can't do? _____ (No, _____ no. _____ No, _____ no.) _____ Is there

an-y-thing im-pos-si-ble? _____ (No, no. _____ No, no.) _____ Will He with-

hold an-y _____ good thing _____ from you? _____ Say it. (No, _____ no. _____ No, _____ no.) _____ Is there

(No, _____ no. _____ No, _____ no.) _____ That which _____ He's spo-ken, He's

faith - ful to ___ per - form. ___ It will come to ___ pass. ___

___ If we be - lieve, ___ and ___ we speak, He can do ___

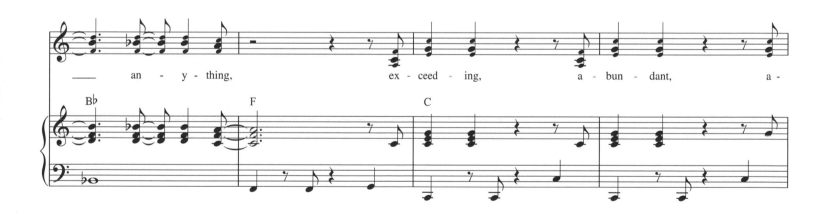

___ an - y - thing, ex - ceed - ing, a - bun - dant, a -

bove all ___ we ask ___ or think. He is a - ble ___

to turn the ta - bles in my fa - vor___ if we're faith-,

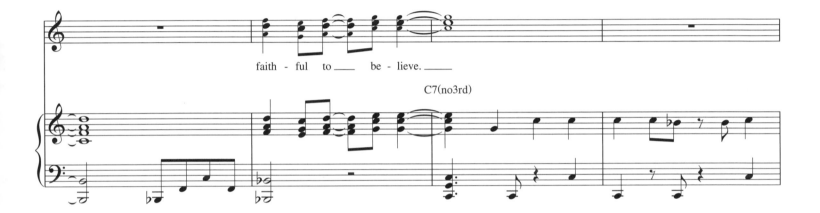

faith - ful to___ be - lieve.___

Is there an - y - thing___ too hard___ for the Lord?

(No, no. ___ No, no.) ___ Is there an-y-thing ___ that He ___ can't ___ do? ___

Is there an-y-thing ___ im-pos - si - ble? ___ Say it.
(No, ___ no. ___ No, ___ no.) ___

(No, no. ___ No, no.) ___ Will He with-hold an-y ___ good thing ___ from you? ___ Well...

(No, ___ no. ___ No, ___ no.) ___ That which ___ He's spo - ken, He's

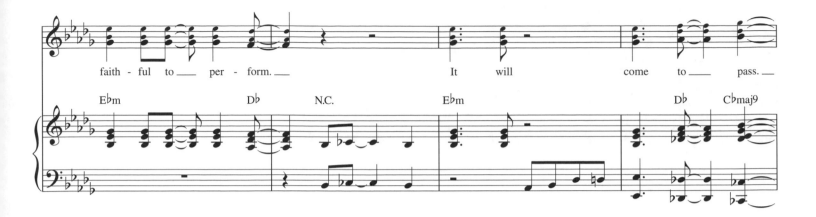

faith - ful to ___ per - form. ___ It will come to ___ pass. ___

___ If we be - lieve, ___ and ___ we speak, He can do ___

___ an - y - thing, ex - ceed - ing, a - bun - dant, a -

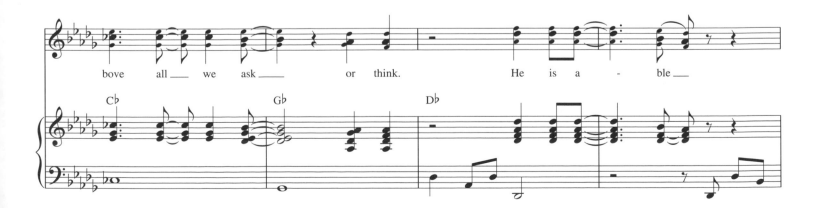

bove all ___ we ask ___ or think. He is a - ble ___

to turn the ta - bles in my fa - vor ___ if we're faith-,

C♭maj7   E♭m11   D♭ C♭maj9

faith - ful to ___ be - lieve. ___ I be - lieve, yes, yes, I do ___ be - lieve.

D♭7(no3rd)

(I be - lieve, yes, yes, I do ___ be - lieve, yeah.) I be - lieve, yes, yes, I do ___ be - lieve.

Do you know you are ___ vic - to - ri - ous? ___

(I be - lieve, yes, yes, I do ___ be - lieve.

C♭ G♭/B♭   C♭ D♭   D   N.C.

(Yeah, yeah. __ Yeah, yeah.) __ And His fa - vor's reign - ing o - ver us. _____

(Yeah, yeah. __ Yeah, yeah.) __ Are His prom - is - es ___ more than ___ e - nough? _ Say:

(Yeah, yeah. __ Yeah, yeah.) __ Are your af - fec - tions set ___ on things ___ a - bove? _ Say:

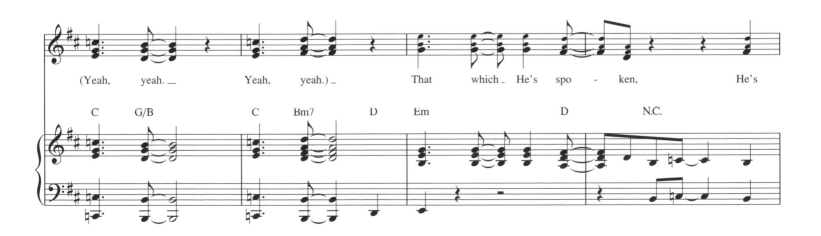

(Yeah, yeah. __ Yeah, yeah.) _ That which __ He's spo - ken, He's

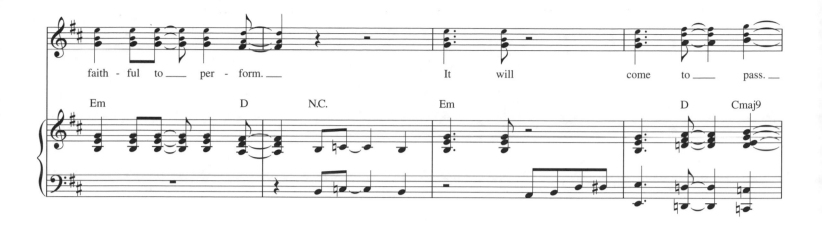

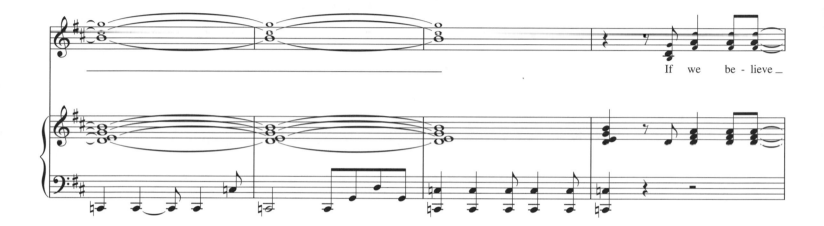

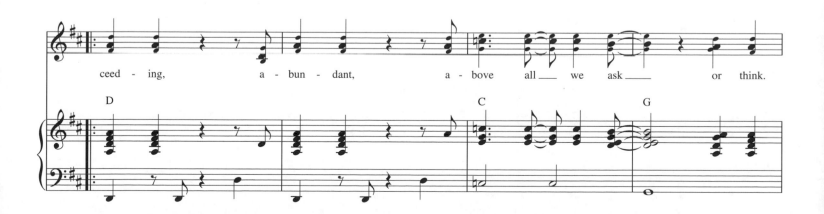

He is a - ble ___ to turn the ta-

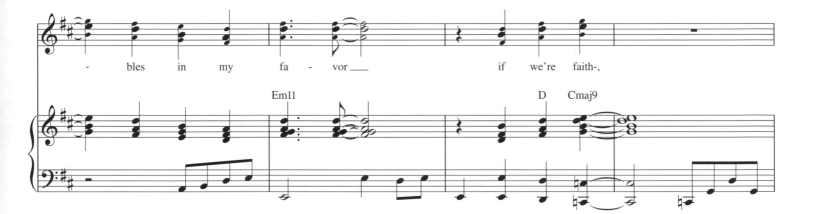

- bles in my fa - vor ___ if we're faith-,

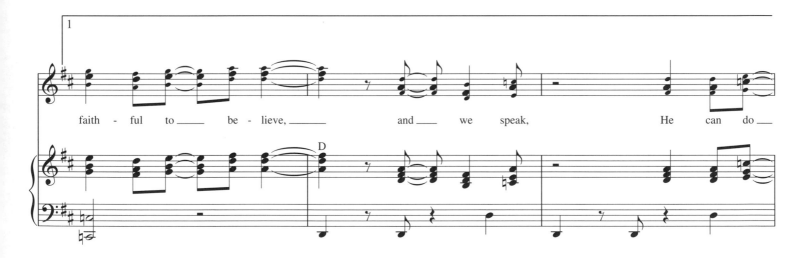

faith - ful to ___ be - lieve, ___ and ___ we speak, He can do ___

___ an - y - thing, ex faith - ful to ___ be - lieve. ___

yes, I do ____ be - lieve.) I be - lieve He's a God who knows ____ the

path in life we're or - dained to go. That means that e - ven if a door should close, some -

where out there, there's a win - dow for sure, o - pened up, big bless - ings that we

can't re - tain, ____ and we got so much we got - ta give it a - way.

(...can't re - tain, ____ and we got so much...)

52

yes, I do __ be - lieve, yeah.) I be - lieve, yes, yes, I do __ be - lieve, yeah. (I be - lieve, yes,

yes, I do __ be - lieve, yeah.) I be - lieve, yes, yes, I do __ be - lieve, yeah. (Yes, yes, yes, yes,

yes, I do __ be - lieve.) And __ we speak, _____ He can do __ an - y - thing, __

ex -

faith - ful to __ be - lieve. __

faith - ful to __ be - lieve.) __

FOREVER

Words and Music by
CECE WINANS

Choir:

Lord, why __ would I leave __ You? __ There's that
I can't __ de - scribe this __ joy __

no oth - er place for __ me __ but here. Your
I feel __ when I'm a - lone __ with You. Your

love is __ so great and __ sure. __ Your
pres - ence, __ it heals my __ soul. __

faith - ful - ness and mer - cy will live __ on e -

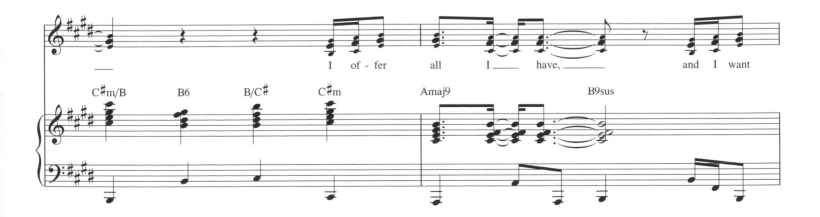

more to ____ give. ____ For-ev-er my life is ____ Yours ____ to use. ____

For - ev - er I'll ____

For - ev - er I'll _

____ live right, for-ev-er I'll ____ love right, __ for-ev-er, for ____ You. ____

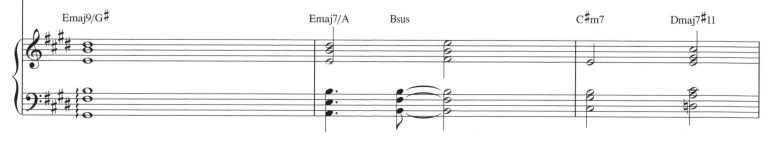

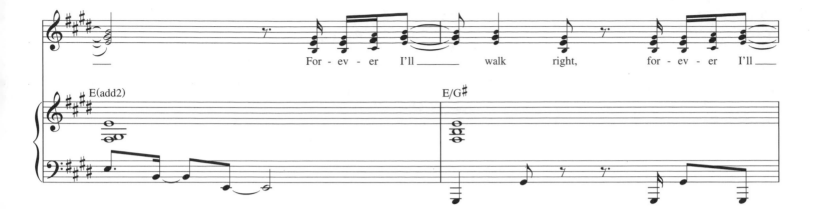

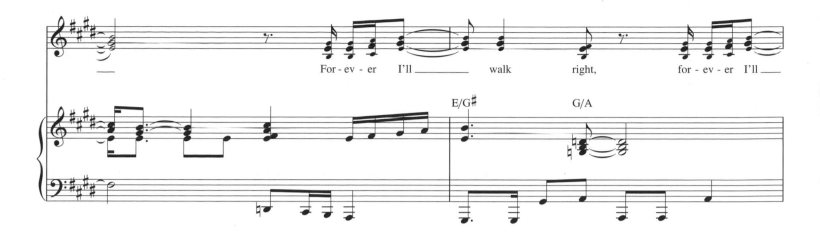

For-ev-er I'll _____ walk right, for-ev-er I'll _____

E/G#   G/A

(Lord, __ You're wor - thy, _____

_____ talk right, for - ev - er, for _____ You. _____

E/B   C#m7   Dmaj9

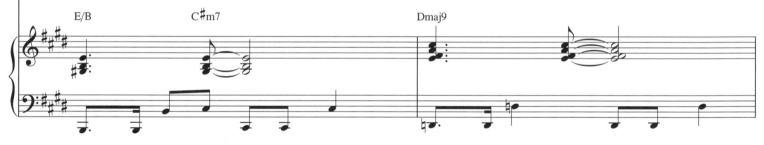

oh, ___ so wor - thy.) _____

For-ev-er I'll _____ live right, for - ev - er I'll _____

E   E/G#

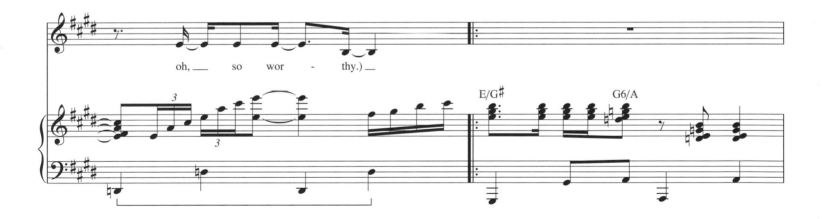

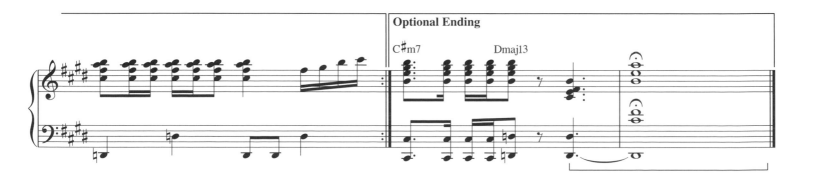

GO WITH ME

Words and Music by ERIC DAWKINS,
WARRYN CAMPBELL and DEITRICK HADDON

Moderately fast

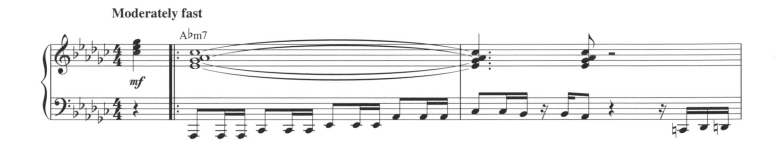

1st time only:

If you're feel-ing like you're stuck in a place that you knew you weren't sup-posed to be in, and you wan-na get

2nd time only:

There's a lot of peo-ple go-ing thru the same thing that you're go-ing thru ev-'ry day, so you're not a-

out, but you got a lit-tle doubt,

lone, no, you're not a - lone. _____

Eᵇm7

and you don't know the first thing to do, but you know you got-ta make a move be-fore the bot-tom falls

But you may nev-er know it, 'cause they ain't gon' show it. It would take a-way from the funk they're

Aᵇm7

out, let me help you out. _____

on, like they've got it un-der con - trol. _____

Eᵇm7

Both times:

You don't have to stay; you can get a - way.

Abm7

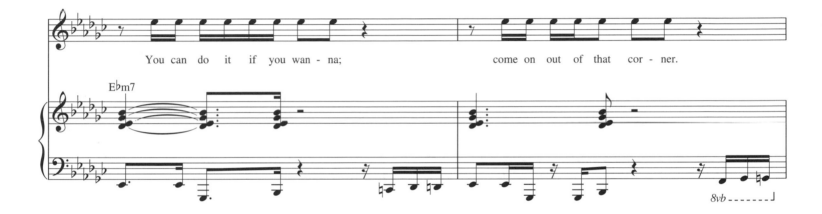

You can do it if you wan - na; come on out of that cor - ner.

Ebm7

8vb

Don't you be a - fraid; come on, where's your faith?

Abm7

Put some work be - hind your faith, and just be - lieve it. Go

Ebm7

8vb

with me.

Both times:

All you got - ta do is put one foot in f

A♭m7

Go

v - 'ry - bod - y's lov - ing each oth - er. _____

8vb _____

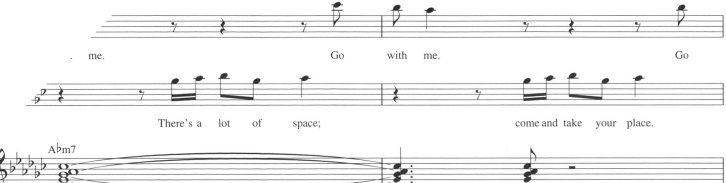

. me.

Go with me.

Go

There's a lot of space; come and take your place.

A♭m7

with me. Come on. ___

Come on, come on, you won't re-gret it. Come on. ___

E♭m7

(You ___ have a choice. ___

you won't re-gret it.

C♭maj9

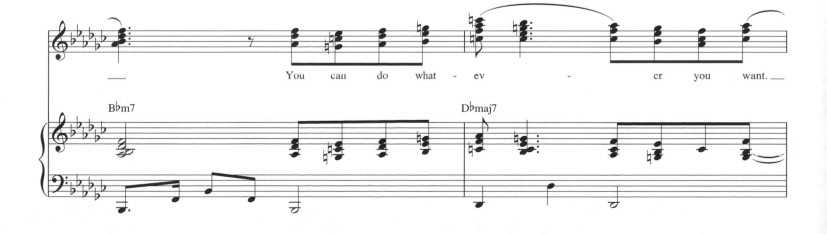

You can do what-ev - er you want. ___

B♭m7

D♭maj7

All it takes is mak - ing up your mind to.)

Cm7   Cm7b5   Cbmaj9   Bbm7

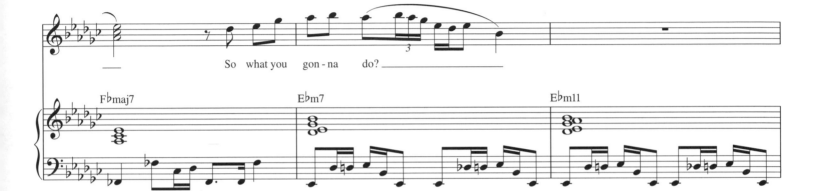

So what you gon - na do?

Fbmaj7   Ebm7   Ebm11

(Go   with

Abm7

8vb

me.   Go   with   me.   Oh,

Ebm7

8vb

go with me. Won't you go with me, go with me, go

A♭m7   E♭m7

with me? Go with me.)

Mm, _____ put one

A♭m7

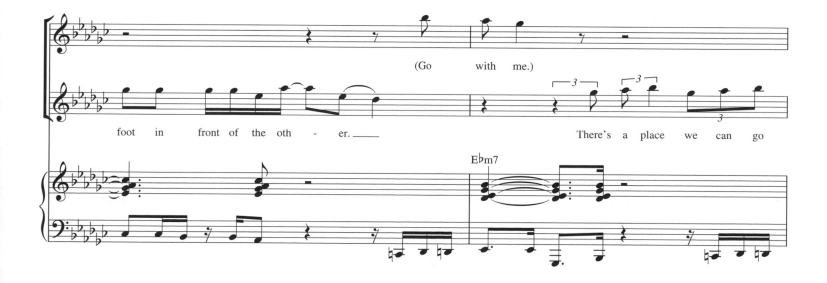

(Go with me.)

foot in front of the oth - er. _____ There's a place we can go

E♭m7

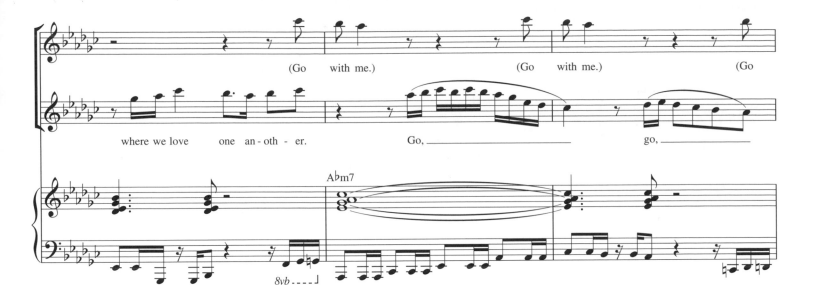

(Go with me.) (Go with me.) (Go

where we love one an - oth - er. Go, _____ go, _____

A♭m7

8vb ----

with me.)

go, ____ go, ____ go. ____ *(Lead vocal ad lib. to end)*

E♭m7

A♭m7

8vb ----

Repeat and Fade

E♭m7

8vb ----

Optional Ending

8vb ------

HAVE A TALK WITH GOD

Words and Music by STEVIE WONDER
and CALVIN HARDAWAY

Moderately slow

There are peo - ple who __ have let __ the prob - lems of __ to - day __
Man - y of __ us feel __ we walk a - lone __ with - out __ a friend; __
Vocal ad lib.

lead them to __ con - clude __ that for __ them life __ is not __ the way. But ev - 'ry
nev - er com - mun - i - cat - ing __ with the one who lives __ with - in. For - get - ting
Vocal ad lib. ends Well, He's the

(1.,3.) When you feel _____ your _____ life's _____ too _____ hard _____
(2.) When your load's _____ too _____ much _____ to _____ bear _____

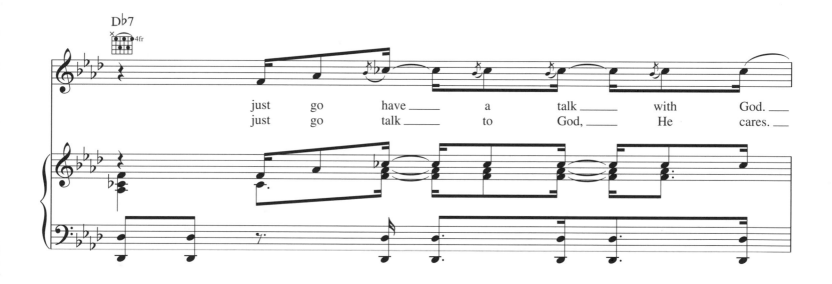

just go have _____ a talk _____ with _____ God. _____
just go talk _____ to God, _____ He cares. _____

Play 3 times

HELP ME BELIEVE

Words and Music by
KIRK FRANKLIN

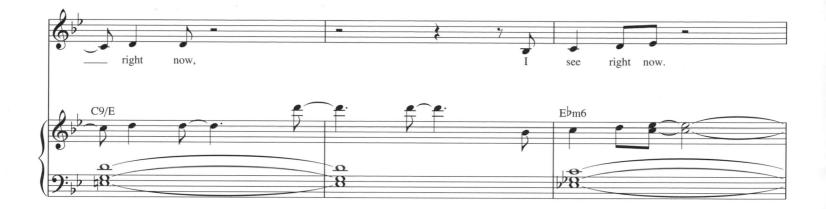

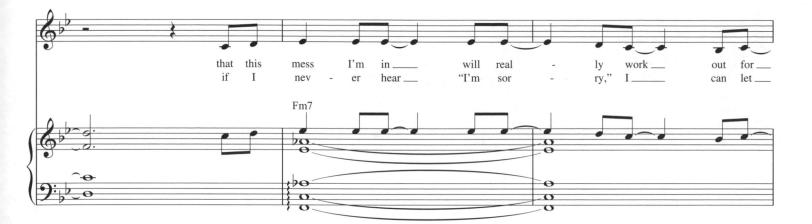

that this mess I'm in ___ will real - ly work ___ out for ___
if I nev - er hear ___ "I'm sor - ry," I ___ can let ___

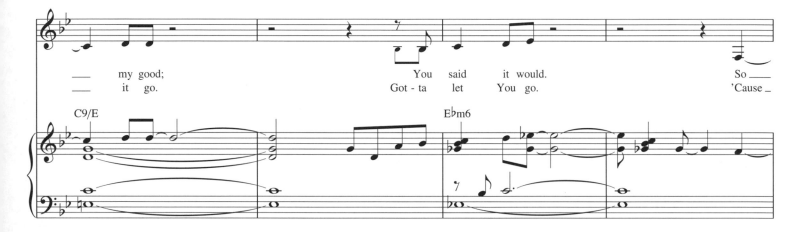

___ my good; You said it would. So ___
___ it go. Got - ta let You go. 'Cause ___

(Harmony 2nd time only)

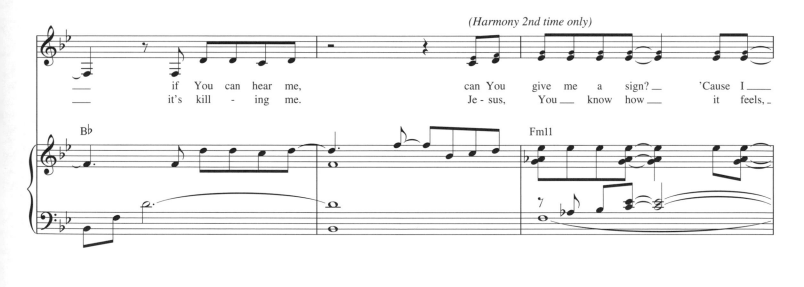

___ if You can hear me, can You give me a sign? ___ 'Cause I ___
___ it's kill - ing me. Je - sus, You ___ know how ___ it feels, ___

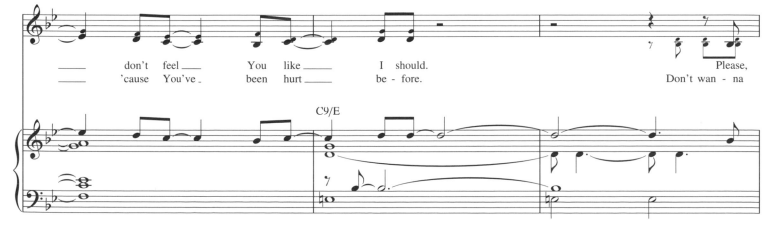

___ don't feel ___ You like ___ I should. Please,
'cause You've ___ been hurt ___ be - fore. Don't wan - na

82

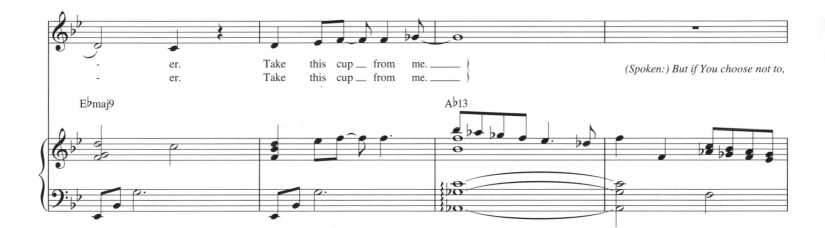

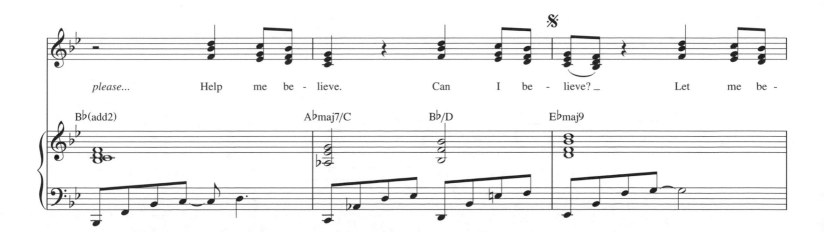

I wan-na be - lieve, ____ be - lieve, ____ be - lieve, _____

F7sus   Bb(add2)   Abmaj9

1. be - lieve. ____   2. be - lieve, ____

Gbmaj9   Cm7/F   Gbmaj9

be - lieve, _____   -ieve, ____

Fm9   Gbmaj9   Ab/Gb   Gbmaj9

be - lieve, _____

Dbmaj13   Gbmaj9

86

o- ver and ___ my work is through, ___ 'cause I be-

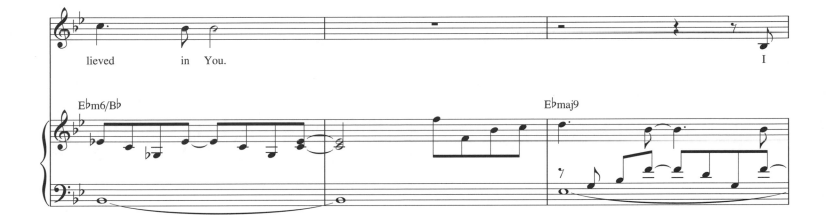

lieved in You. I

know dark nights ___ will come, ___ and some days there'll be ___ no sun -

- shine, and You're too far ___ to see. ___

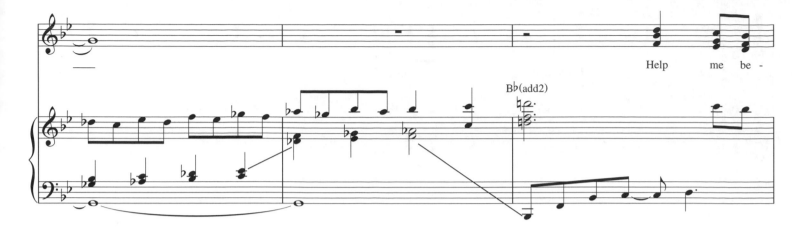

Help me be-

D.S. al Coda

CODA

lieve. Can I be -

I wan-na be-lieve, _____ be-lieve, _____

Lead vocal ad lib. (spoken)

Abmaj7/C   Bb/D

F7sus   Bb(add2)

be - lieve, _____   be - lieve, _____   be - lieve, __

Abmaj9   Gbmaj9   Cm7/F

be - lieve, __   be - lieve, __   be - lieve, __

Bb(add2)   Abmaj9   Gbmaj9

be - lieve, _____ be - lieve, _____ be - lieve, _____ be - lieve, __

Cm7/F   B♭   A♭maj9   G♭maj9

be - lieve, _____ be - lieve, _____ be - lieve, _____ be - lieve, __

Cm7/F   Gm11   A♭maj9   G♭maj9

be - lieve, _____ be - lieve, _____ be - lieve, _____ be - lieve, __

Cm7/F   B♭   A♭maj9   G♭maj9

be - lieve, _____ be - lieve, _____ be - lieve, _____ be - lieve, __

Cm7/F   Gm11   A♭maj9   G♭maj9

be - lieve, ____ be - lieve, ____ be - lieve, ____ be - lieve, ____

Cm7/F   B♭   A♭maj9   G♭maj9

be - lieve, ____ be - lieve, ___ be - lieve, ___ be - lieve, _

Cm7/F   Gm11   A♭maj9   G♭maj9

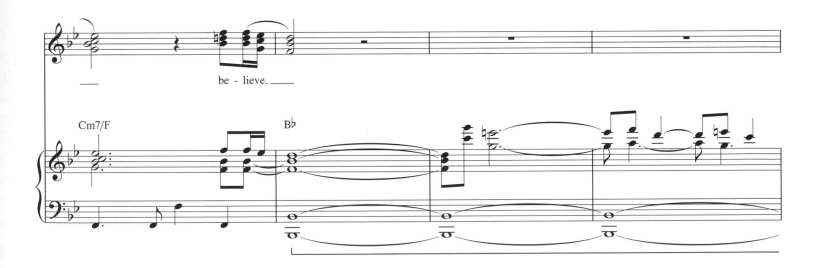

be - lieve. ____

Cm7/F   B♭

I DO WORSHIP

Words and Music by
JOHN P. KEE

For Your good - ness and ___ Your glo - ry, for the

joy in - side ___ Your sto - ry, I do ___

wor - ship You. ___

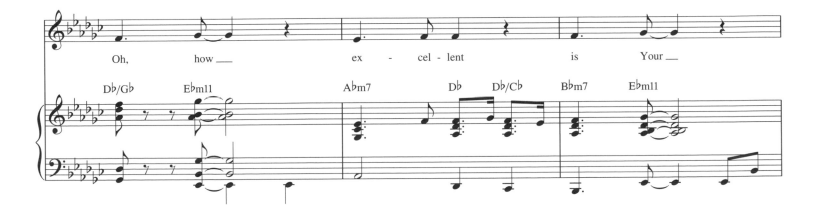

Oh, how ___ ex - cel - lent is Your ___

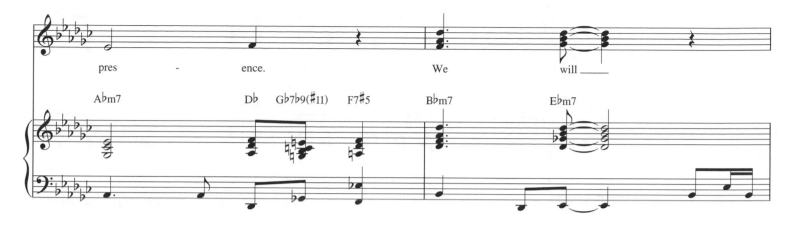

pres - ence. We will ____

A♭m7 D♭ G♭7♭9(♯11) F7♯5 B♭m7 E♭m7

bless Your name.

A♭m7 D♭ G♭ G♭13 E♭m11/G♭ C♭m/G♭

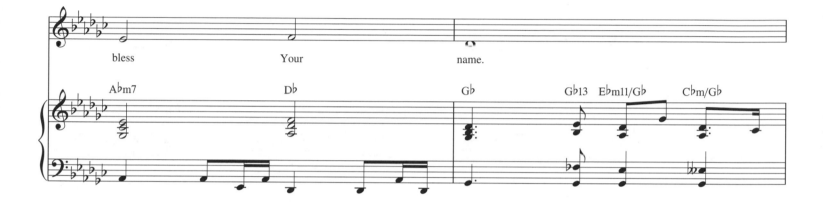

For Your good - ness and ___ Your glo - ry, for the

G♭(add2) E♭m9 A♭7♯5 D♭m9 G♭13sus G♭13♯11

joy in - side ___ Your sto - ry, for the peace You gave ___ to me,

C♭maj9 E9 E♭m11 A♭7♯5 D♭m9

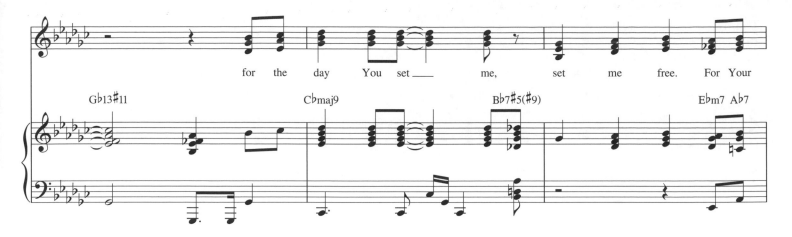

for the day You set ____ me, set me free. For Your

good - ness and ____ Your glo - ry, for the joy in - side ____ Your sto -

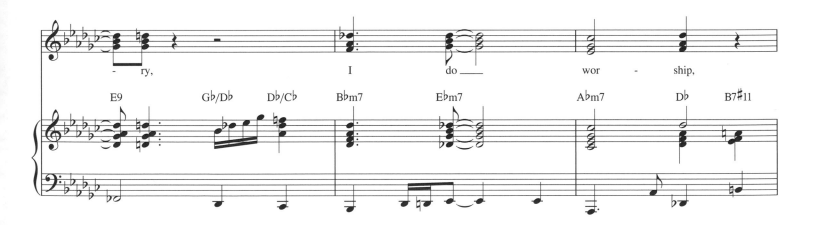

- ry, I do ____ wor - ship,

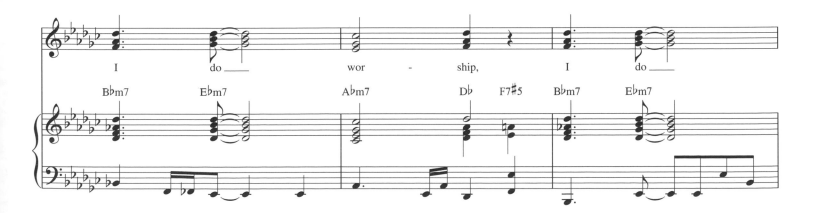

I do ____ wor - ship, I do ____

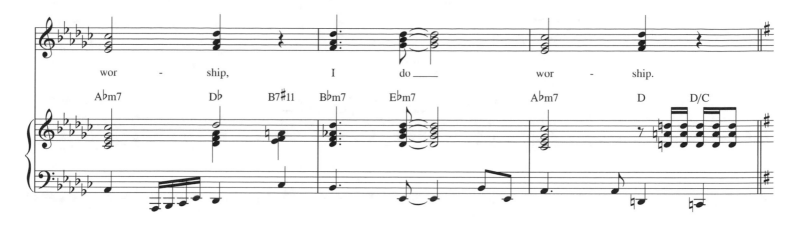

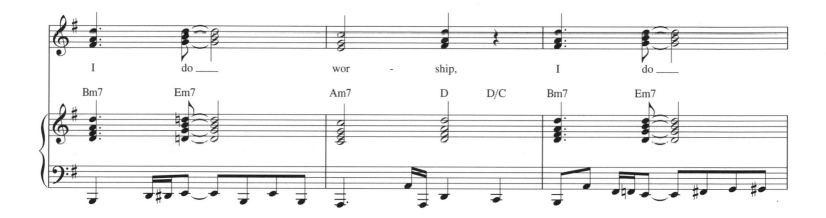

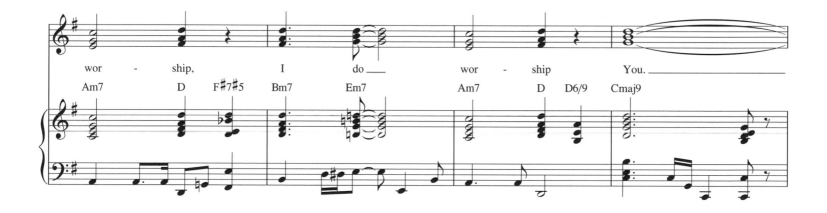

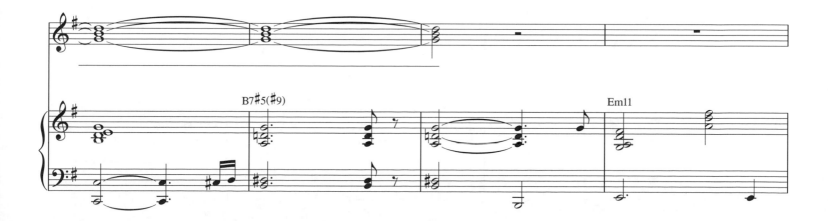

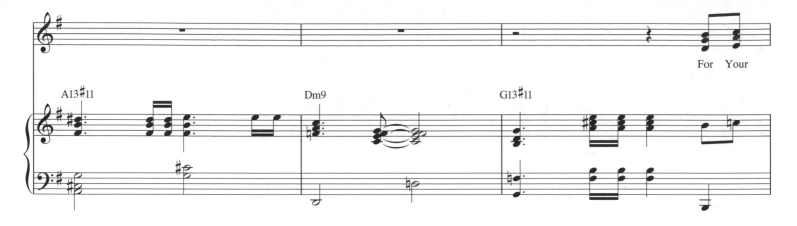

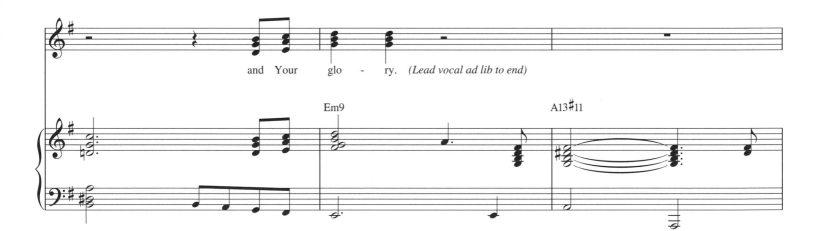

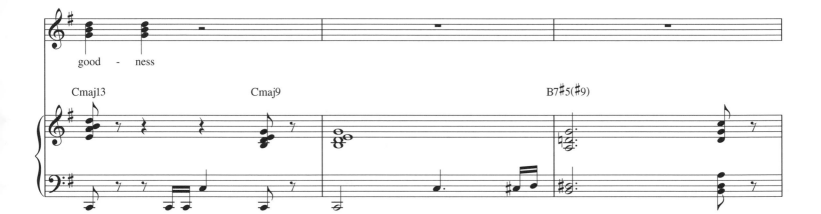

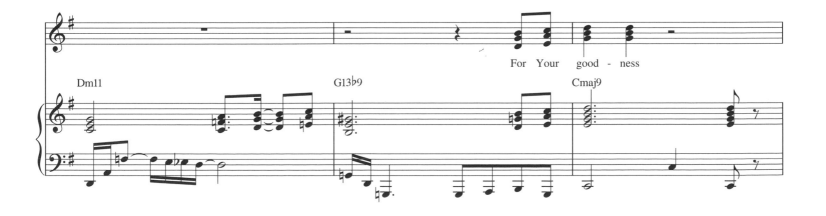

and Your

glo - ry, Hal - le - lu, hal - le - lu, hal - le - lu - jah! _____

He's so faith - ful.

He's so faith - ful.

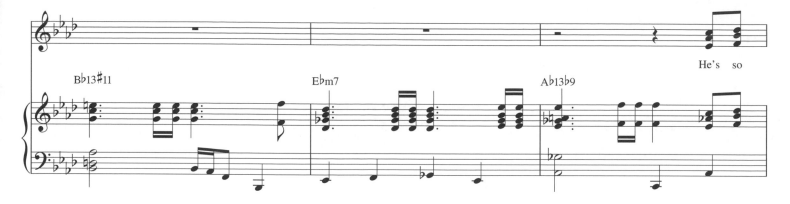

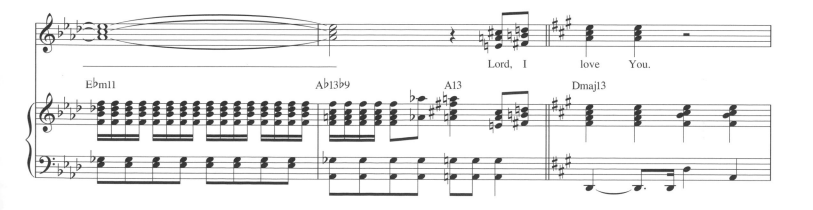

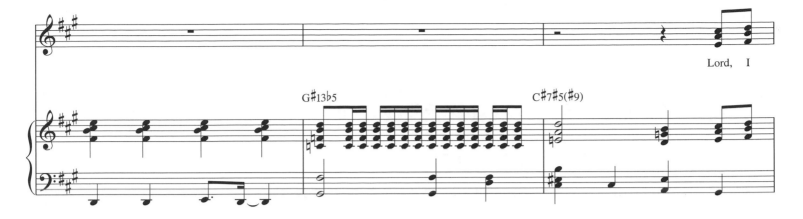

GOD IN ME

Words and Music by WARRYN CAMPBELL,
ERICA ATKINS-CAMPBELL and TRECINA "TINA" CAMPBELL

I LOOK TO YOU

Words and Music by
ROBERT KELLY

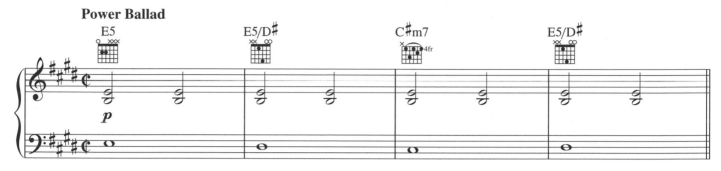

Power Ballad

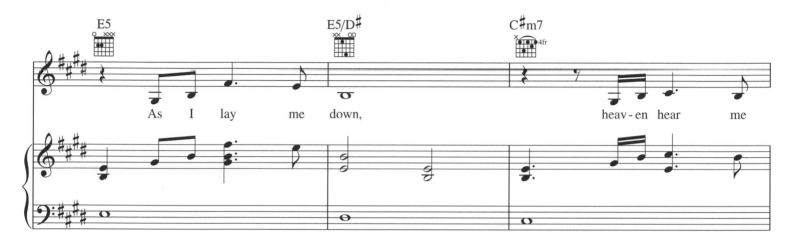

come and dark - ened my _____ sun. _____

Af - ter all _____ that I've been through, _____ who on earth can I turn _____

_____ to? I look to You, _____ I look

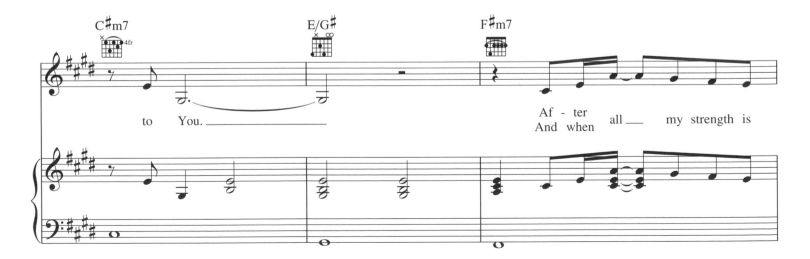

to You. _____

Af - ter all _____ my strength is
And when all _____ my strength is

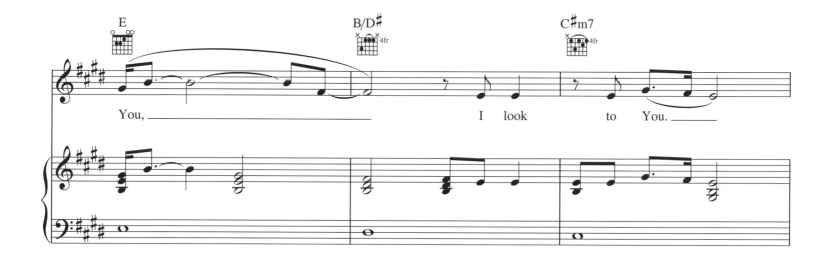

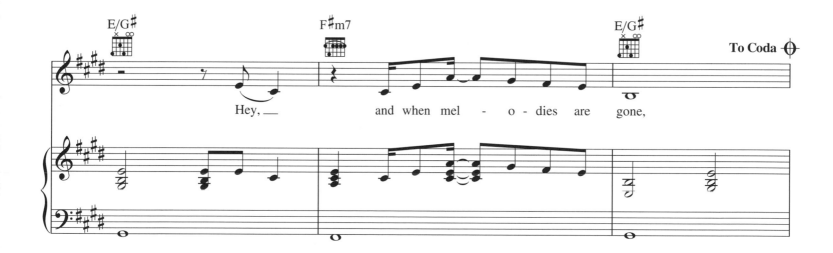

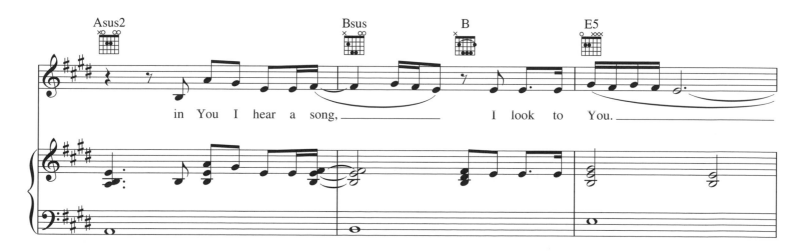

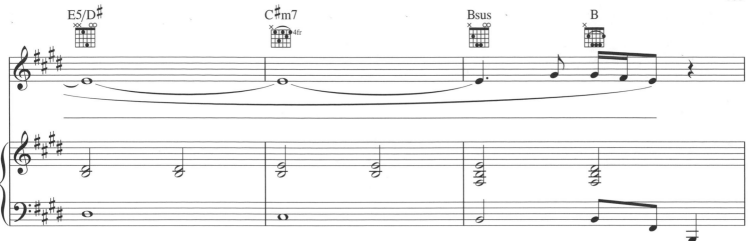

'Bout to lose my breath, _____ there's no more fight - ing

left. _____ Sink - ing to rise _ no more, _____

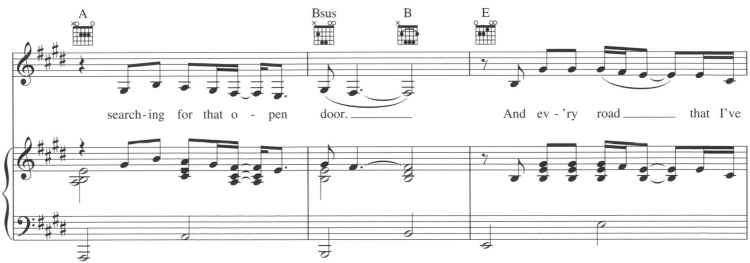

search-ing for that o - pen door. _____ And ev - 'ry road _____ that I've

tak - en _____ led to my _ re - gret. _____

And I don't know if I'm _ gon' make it, _____

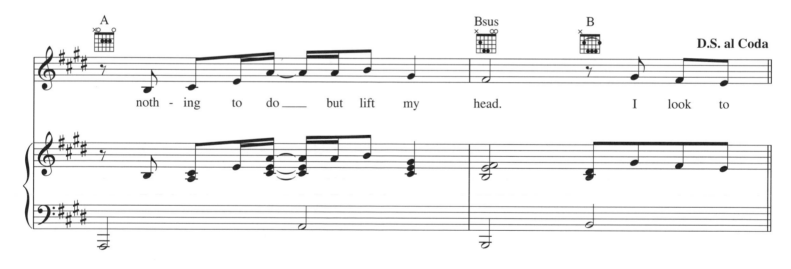

noth - ing to do _ but lift my head. I look to

D.S. al Coda

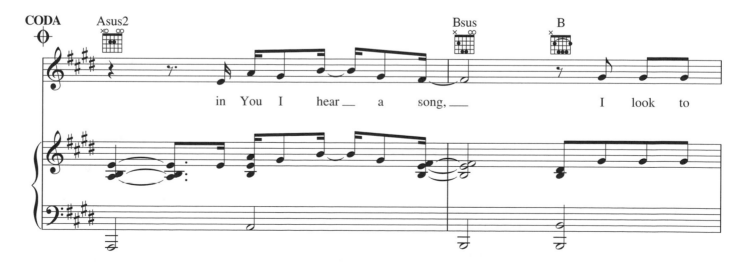

in You I hear _ a song, _ I look to

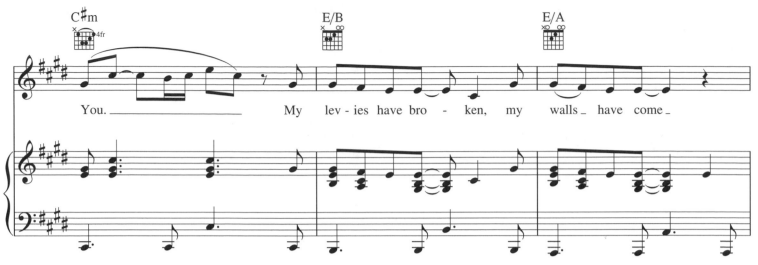

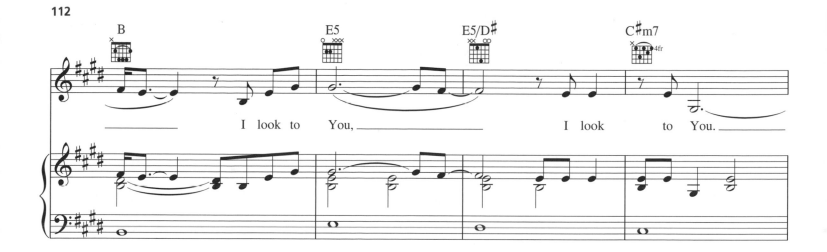

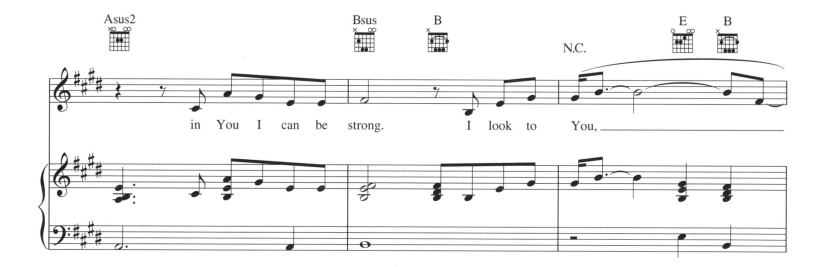

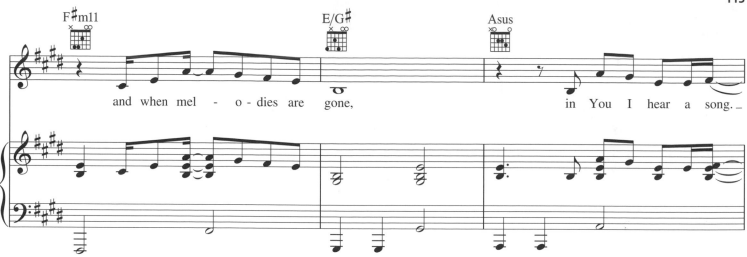

and when mel - o - dies are gone, in You I hear a song.

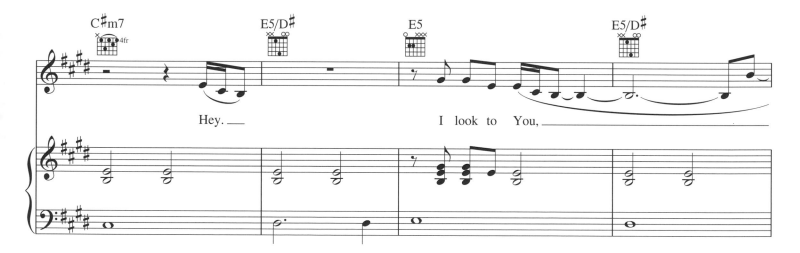

I look to You.

Hey. I look to You,

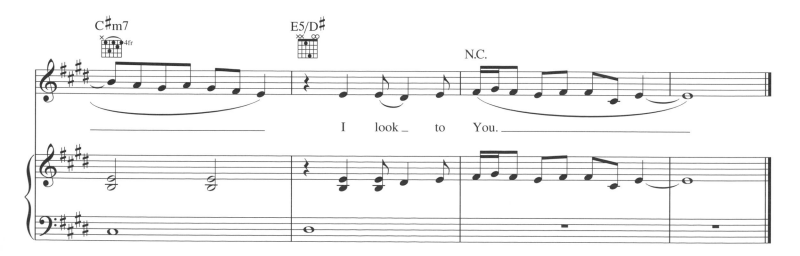

I look to You.

I WISH

Words and Music by
NICOLE C. MULLEN

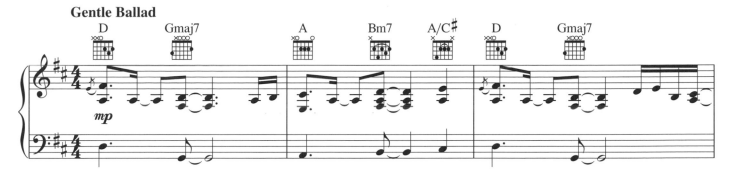

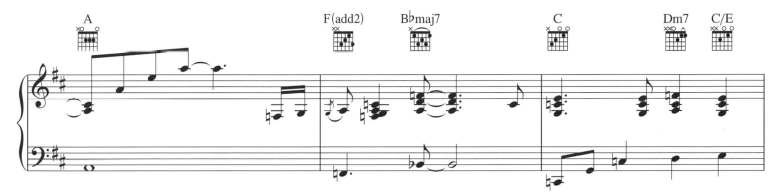

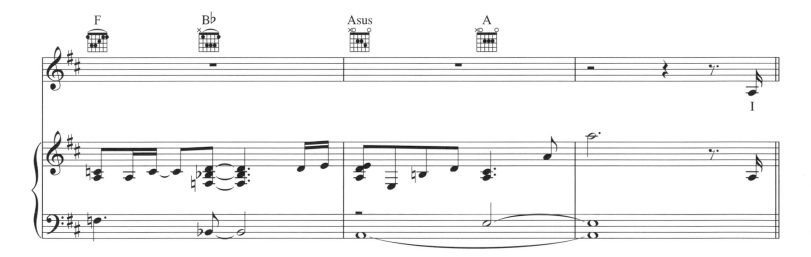

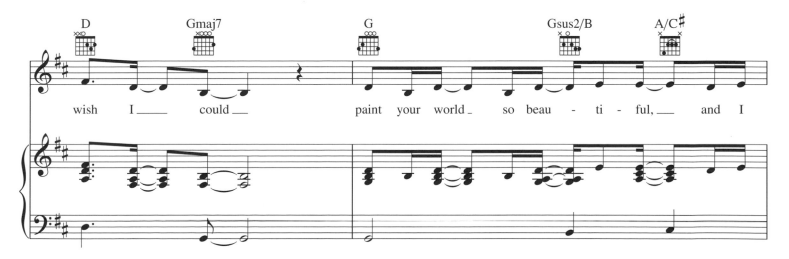

wish I___ could___ paint your world_ so beau - ti - ful,___ and I

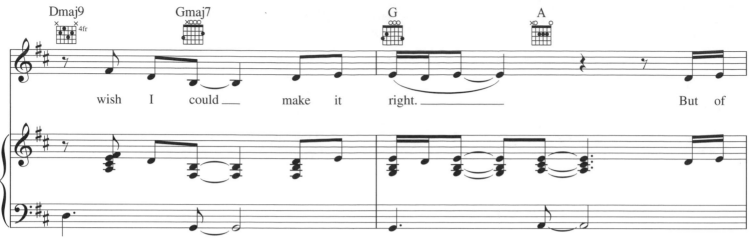

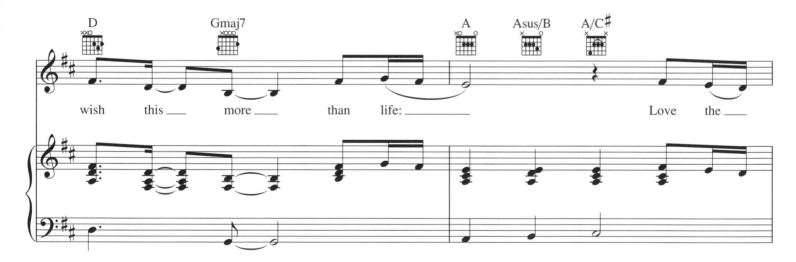

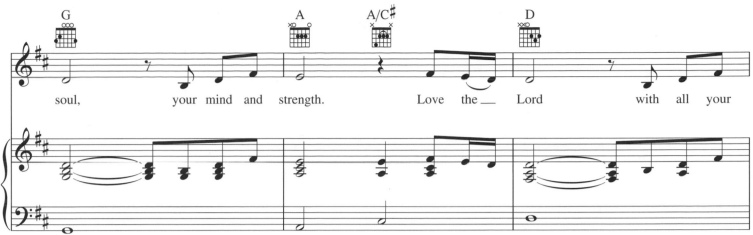

soul,   your mind and strength.   Love the __ Lord   with all your

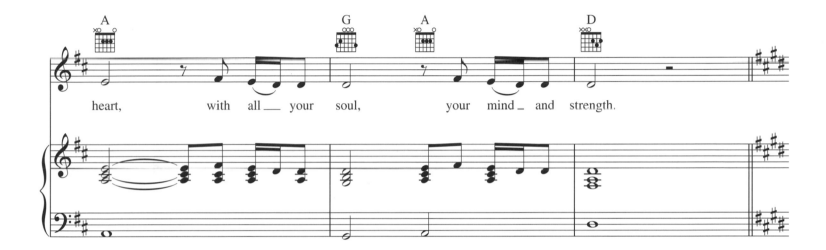

heart,   with all __ your soul,   your mind __ and strength.

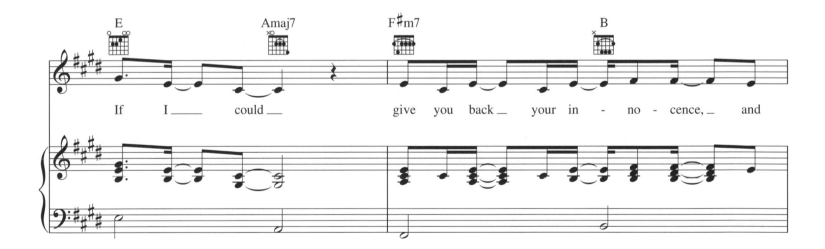

If I __ could __   give you back __ your in - no - cence, __ and

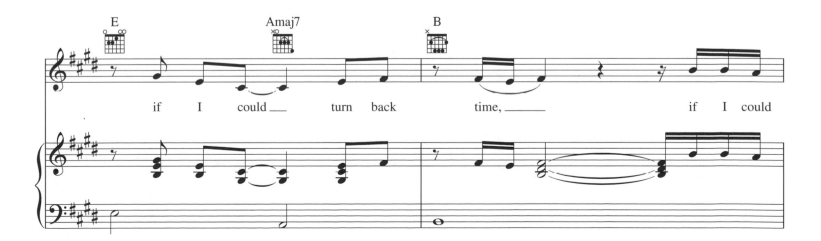

if I could __ turn back   time, _____   if I could

heal you __ of _____ all the bro - ken prom - is - es, ___ still, the

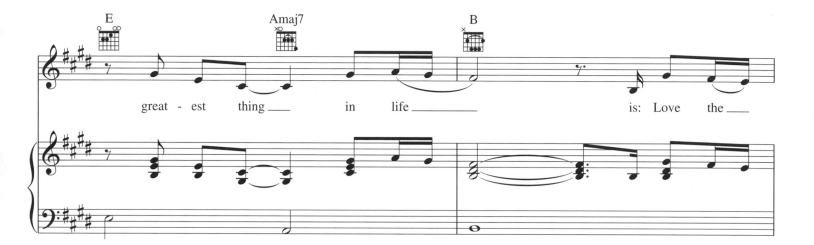

great - est thing ___ in life _____ is: Love the ___

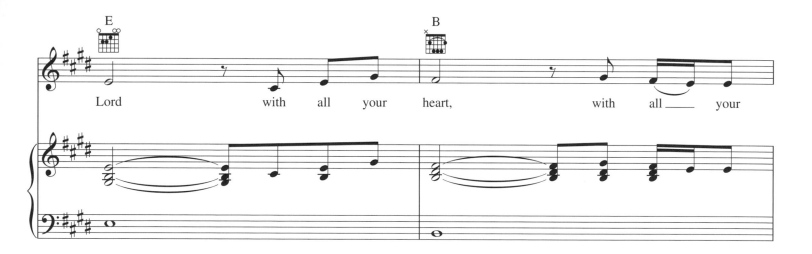

Lord with all your heart, with all ___ your

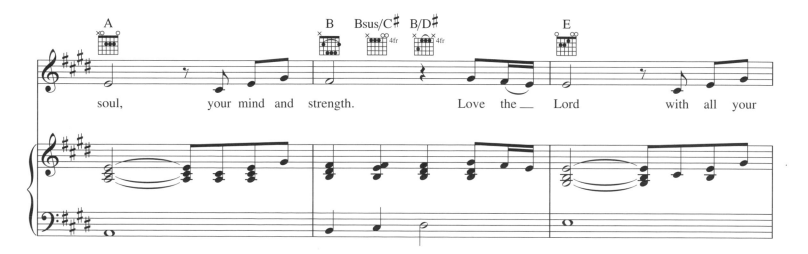

soul, your mind and strength. Love the __ Lord with all your

118

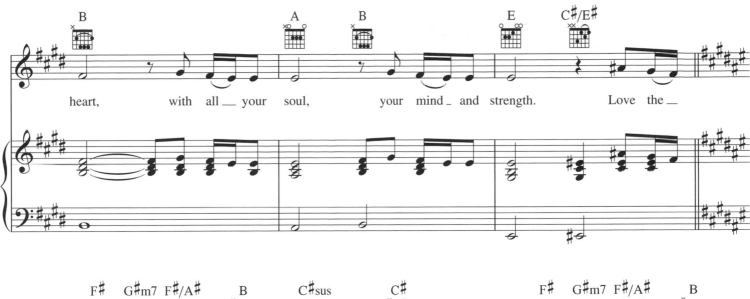

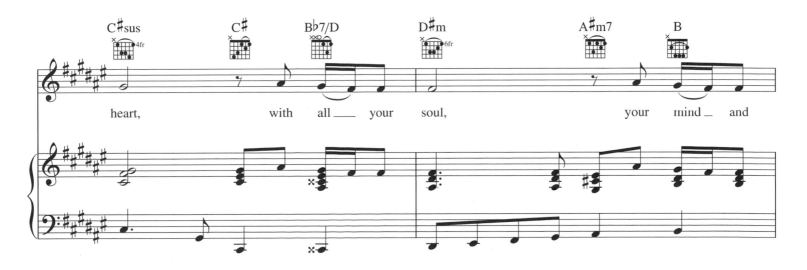

IN THE SANCTUARY

Words and Music by
KURT CARR

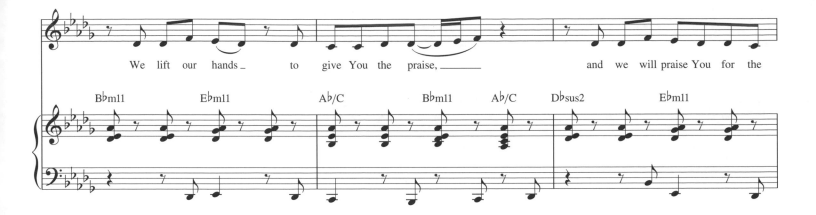

We lift our hands _ to give You the praise, _____ and we will praise You for the

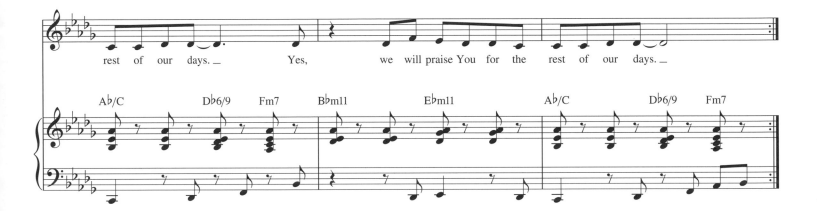

rest of our days. _ Yes, we will praise You for the rest of our days. _

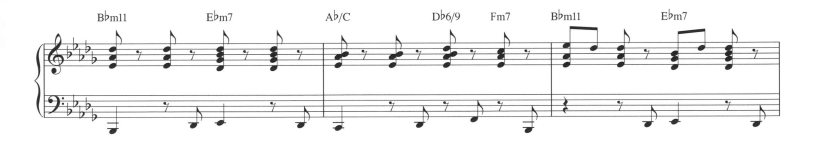

We clap our hands in the sanc - tu - ar - y.

We clap our hands to give You the glo - ry. We clap our hands _ to

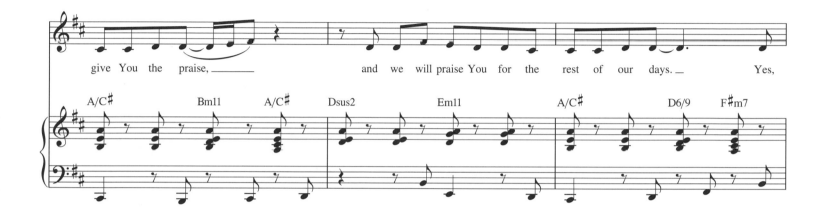

give You the praise, _____ and we will praise You for the rest of our days. _ Yes,

we will praise You for the rest of our days. _ *(Spoken:) Come on, clap your hands, all ye people...*

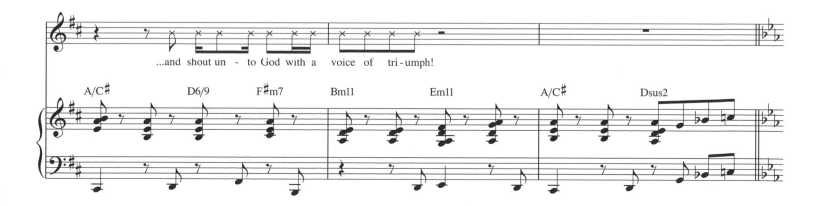

...and shout un - to God with a voice of tri - umph!

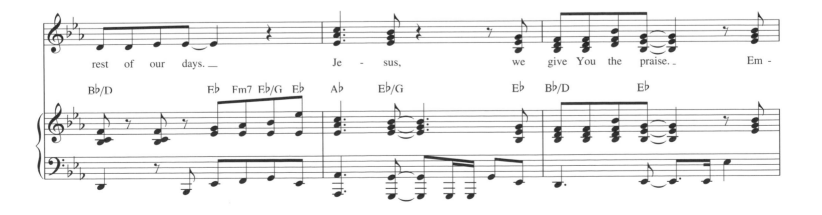

124

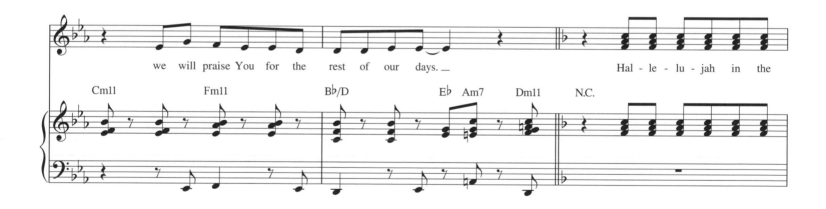

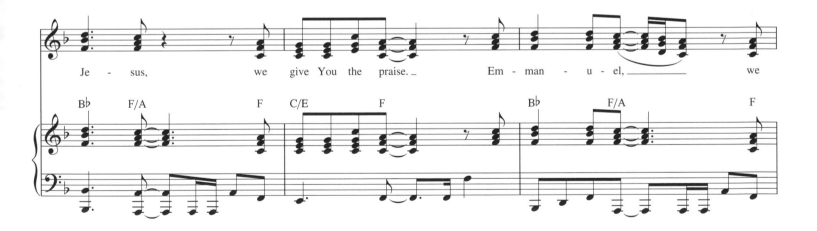

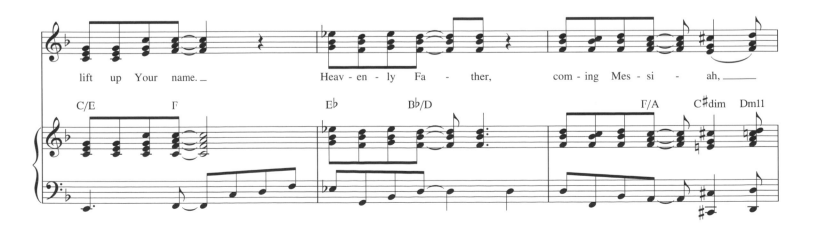

and we will praise You for the rest of our days. ___ Yes, we will praise You for the

rest of our days. ___ *Sopranos:* Yes!

Yes, Lord, for the rest of our days. ___ *Altos:* Yes!

Yes, Lord, for the rest of our days. ___

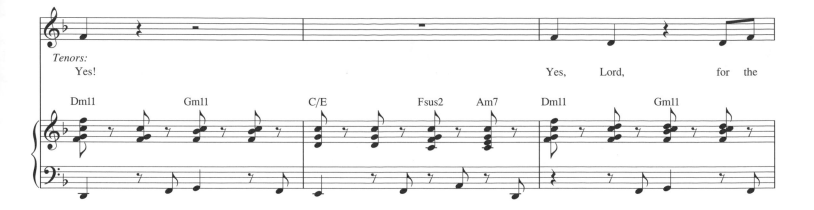

Tenors: Yes! Yes, Lord, for the

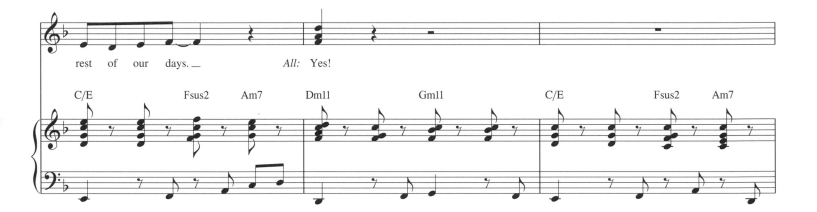

rest of our days. ___ All: Yes!

Yes, Lord, for the rest of our days. ___ Yes!

Yes, Lord, for the rest of our days. ___

128

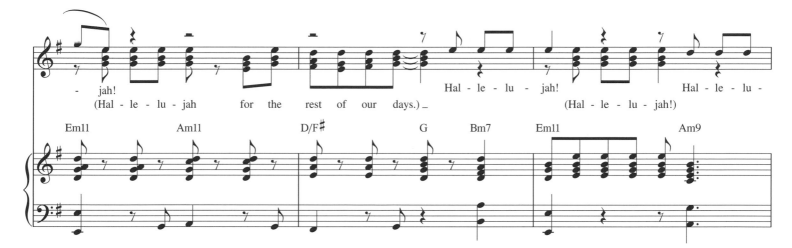

rest of our days.) _   Yes!   Yes, Lord,   for the

Eb/G   Ab(add2)   F#m11   Bm11   E/G#   Asus2   C#m7   F#m11   Bm11

rest of our days. _   And we will praise You for the   rest of our days. _

E/G#   Asus2 C#m7   F#m7   N.C.   E   F#m7 E/G#   A

Yes!   Yes,   Lord,   for the

Gm11   Cm11   F/A   Bbsus2   Dm7   Gm11   Cm11

rest of our days. _   And we will praise You for the   rest of our days. _

F/A   Bbsus2 Dm7   Gm7   N.C.   F   Gm7 F/A   Bb

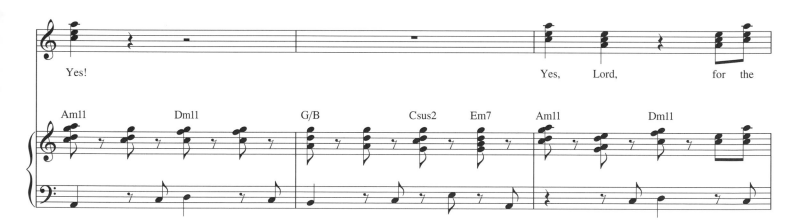

JESUS IS LOVE

Words and Music by
LIONEL RICHIE

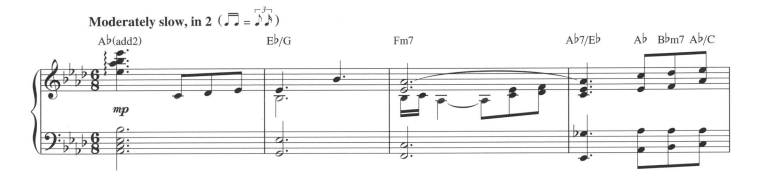

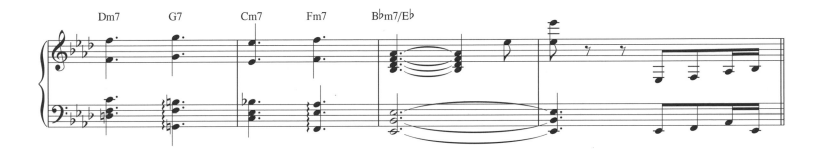

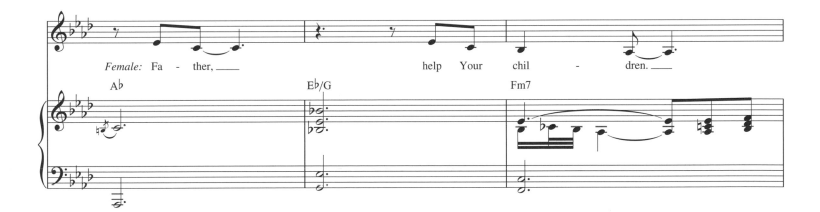

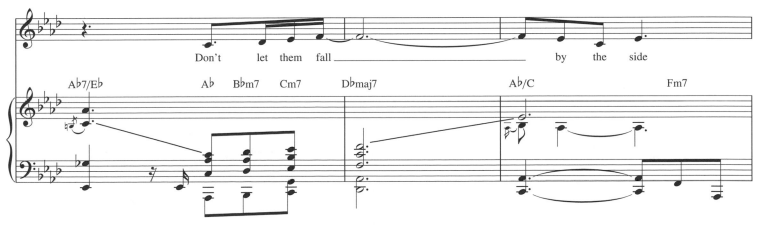

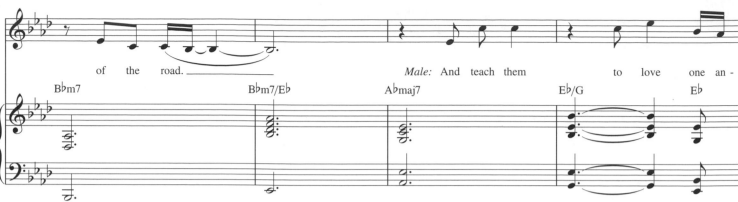

of the road. _____ *Male:* And teach them to love one an-

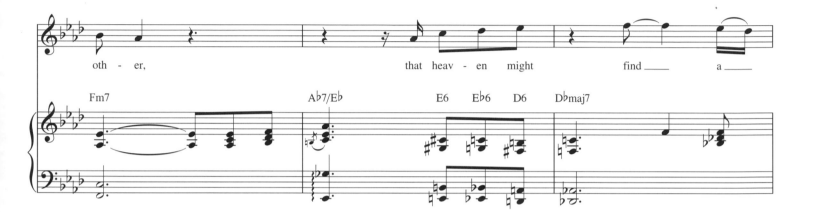

oth - er, that heav - en might find _____ a _____

place in their heart. _____ *Female:* 'Cause Je -

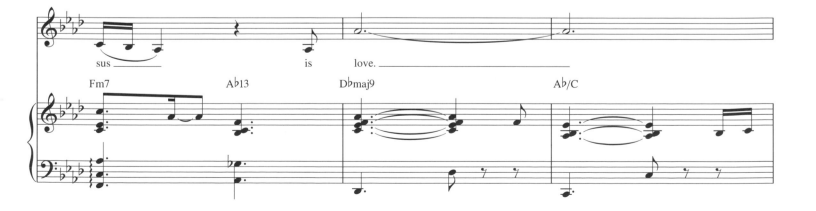

sus _____ is love. _____

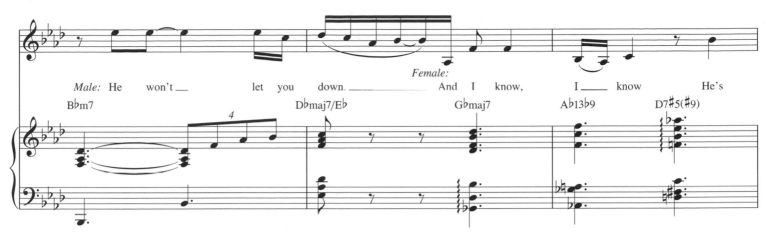

Male: He won't ___ let you down. ___ *Female:* And I know, I ___ know He's

B♭m7   D♭maj7/E♭   G♭maj7   A♭13♭9   D7♯5(♯9)

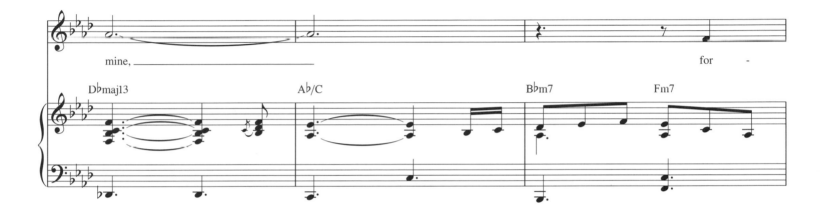

mine, ___ for -

D♭maj13   A♭/C   B♭m7   Fm7

ev - er ___ in my heart.

B♭m7/E♭   A♭maj7   E♭sus

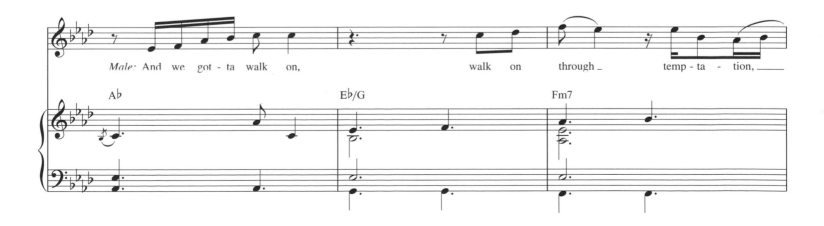

Male: And we got - ta walk on, walk on through ___ temp - ta - tion, ___

A♭   E♭/G   Fm7

'cause His love _____ and His wis-dom will

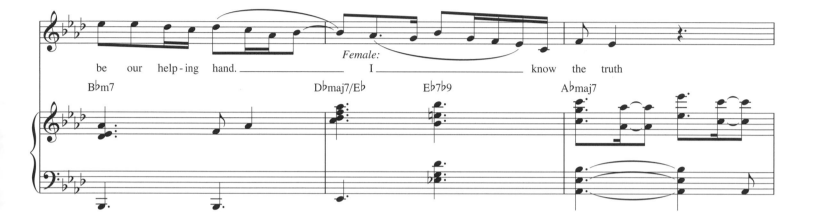

be our help-ing hand. _____ *Female:* I _____ know the truth

and His words, _____ they _____ will be our sal-va - tion. Lift

up our ___ hearts _____ to be thank-ful and glad _____

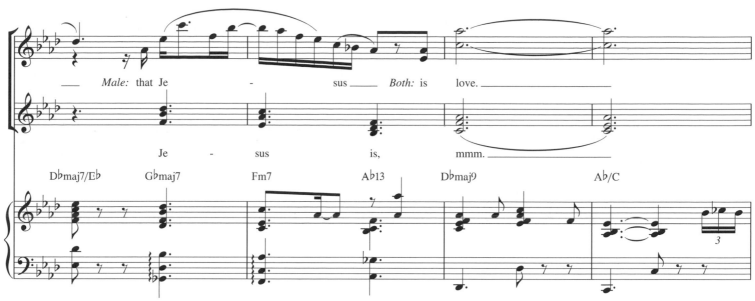

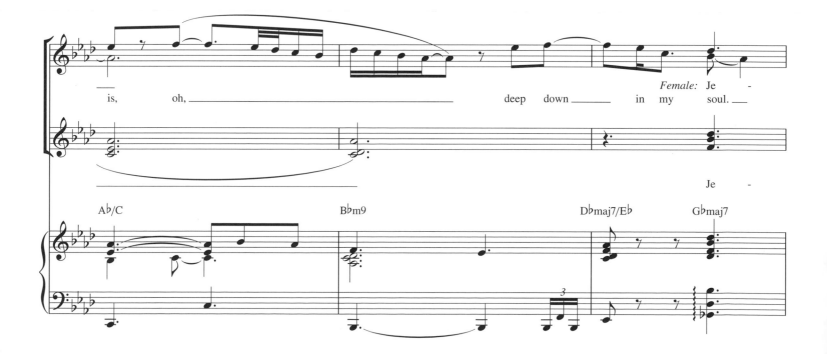

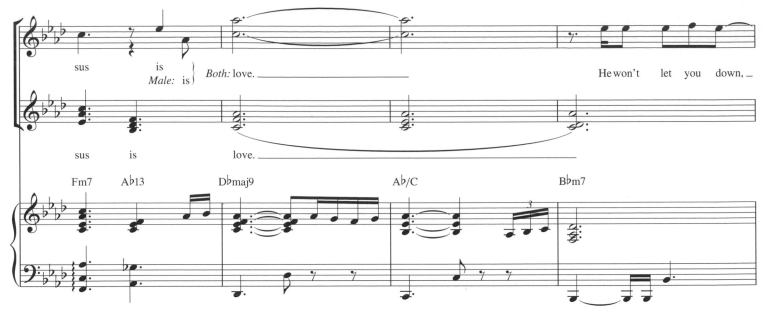

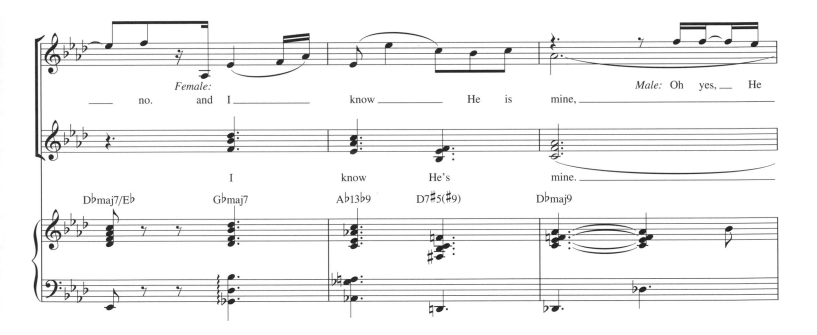

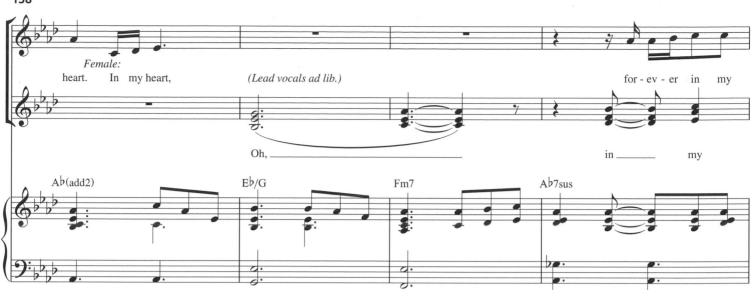

Female:
heart. In my heart, *(Lead vocals ad lib.)* for - ev - er in my
Oh, _____ in _____ my

heart. *Male:* I know. _ *Female:* I know, I know _____ His
heart. _____ Ooh. _____

love is pow - er, His love is glo - ry for - ev - er and ev - er.
Pow - er, glo - ry, ev - er and ev - er and

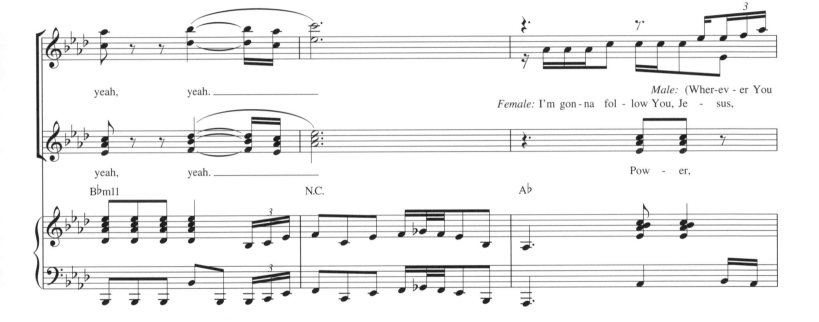

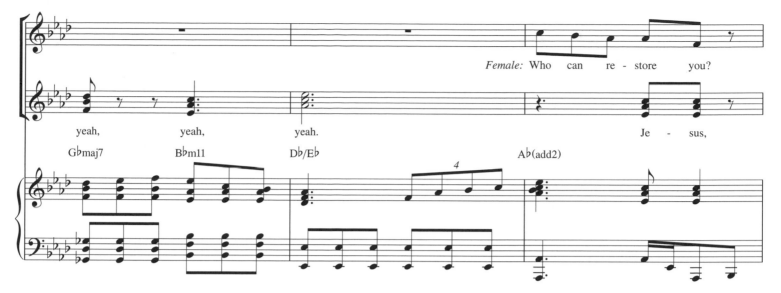

JUSTIFIED

Words and Music by
SMOKIE NORFUL

love made ___ it right. Now what great - er sign ___ can

came _____ and saved me. When the en - e - my said _____ that I ___ could - n't, God said,

F#dim7   Gm9   Bb/D   Ebmaj7

an - y man _____ show, than with his own ___ blood? _____

"Go a - head, _____ be - cause you're

F#dim7   Gm9   Ab13#11

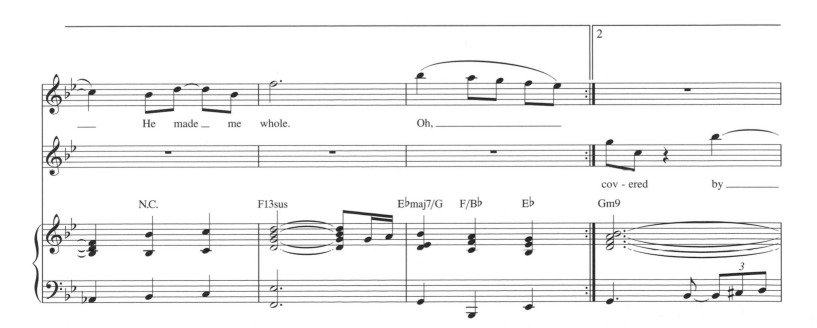

___ He made ___ me whole. Oh, _____

cov - ered by _____

N.C.   F13sus   Ebmaj7/G F/Bb Eb   Gm9

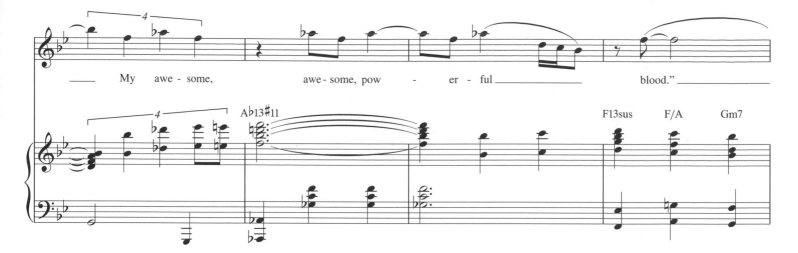

My awe-some, awe-some, pow - er-ful _____ blood." _____

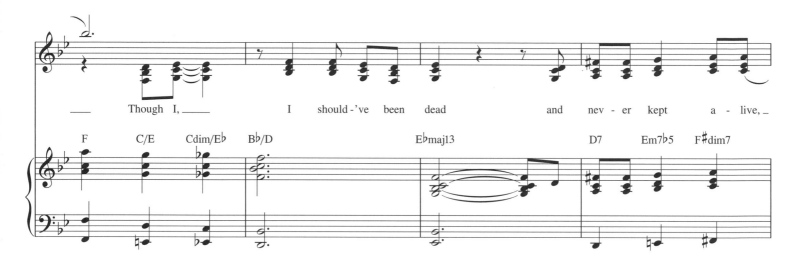

_____ Though I, _____ I should -'ve been dead _____ and nev - er kept a - live, _____

_____ God's grace _____ and His mer - cy _____ were on ev - 'ry side.

When it _____ looks like I can't, _____ God says I can.

been, if it had not been, if it had not been, if it had not been, if it had not been for the

Lord that was on my side. Hey. __ *(Spoken:) Listen. I got some testimonies. Listen.* Just like Nin-

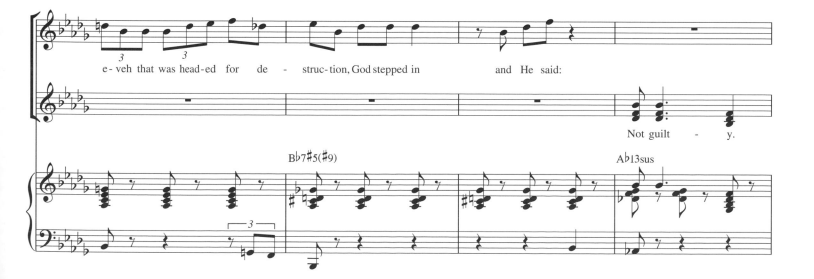

e - veh that was head-ed for de - struc-tion, God stepped in and He said:

Not guilt - y.

150

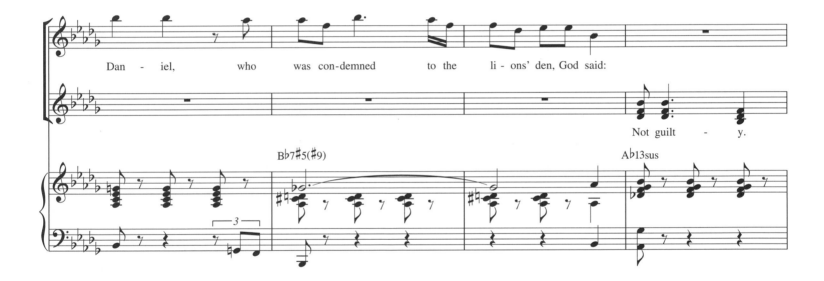

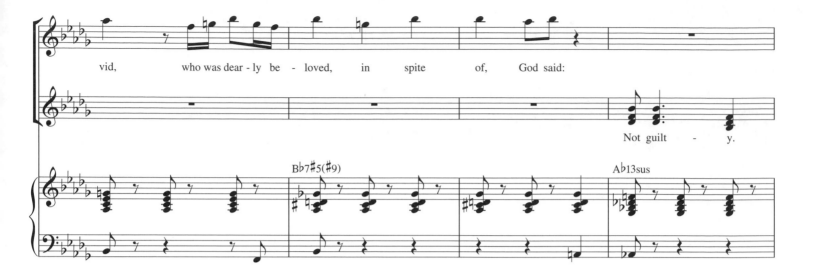

vid,   who was dear - ly be - loved,   in   spite   of,   God said:

Not guilt - y.

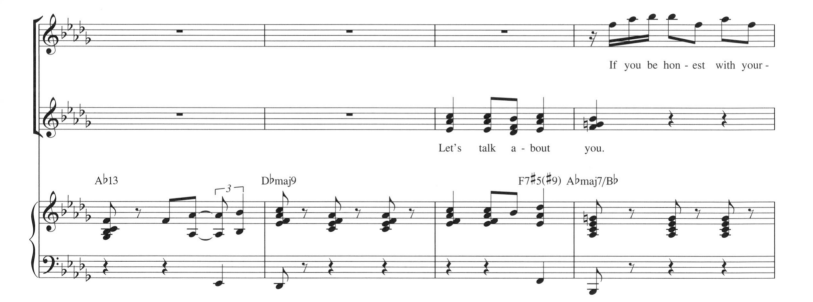

If you be hon - est   with your -

Let's   talk   a - bout   you.

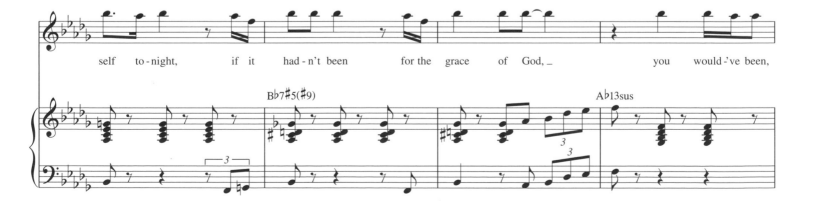

self to - night,   if it   had - n't been   for the   grace   of God, _   you   would - 've been,

153

156

tes - ti - fy. _____ One more time, ___ let your

God did it.

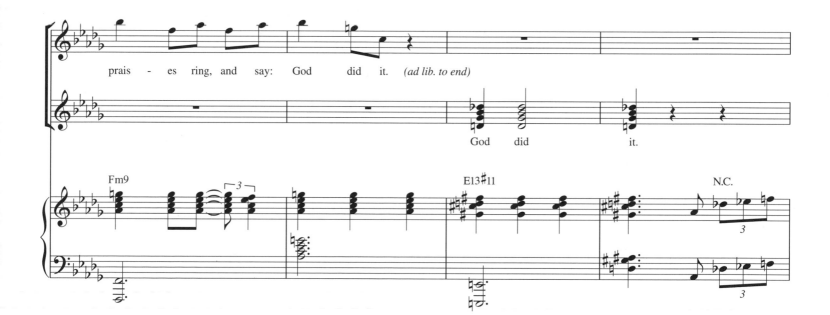

prais - es ring, and say: God did it. *(ad lib. to end)*

God did it.

God did it.

God did it.

NOW BEHOLD THE LAMB

Words and Music by
KIRK FRANKLIN

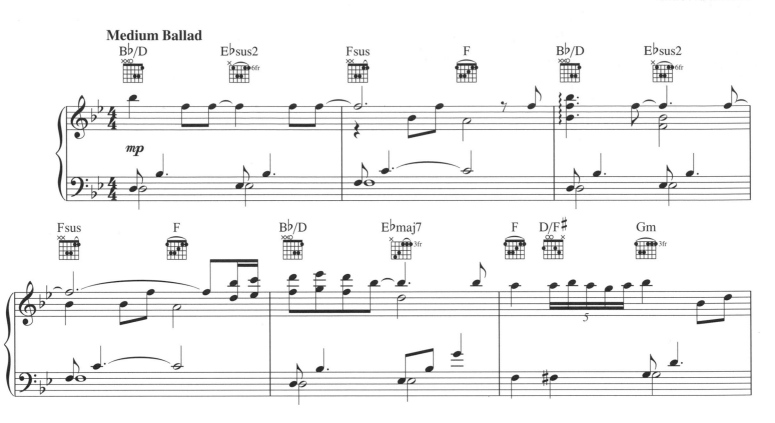

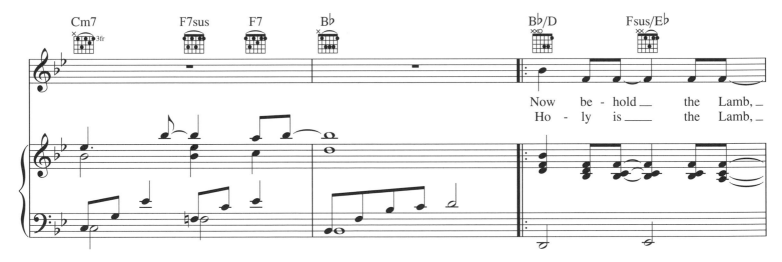

Now be-hold __ the Lamb, __
Ho - ly is ___ the Lamb, __

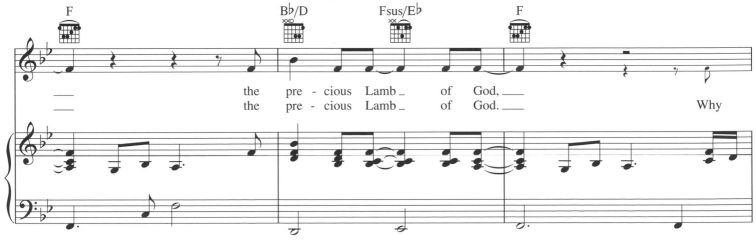

___ the pre - cious Lamb _ of God, ___
___ the pre - cious Lamb _ of God. ___   Why

born in-to sin ___ that I may ___ live a-gain, ___ the pre-cious Lamb ___ of God. ___
You loved me so, ___ Lord, I shall ___ nev-er know, ___ the pre-cious Lamb ___ of God. ___

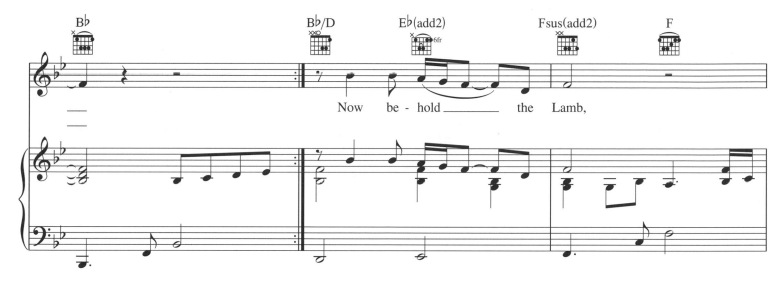

___ Now be-hold ___ the Lamb,

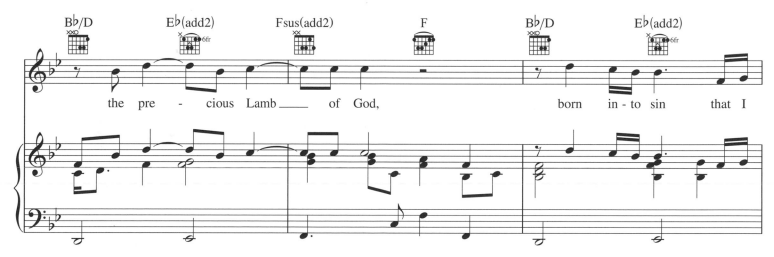

the pre - cious Lamb ___ of God, born in-to sin that I

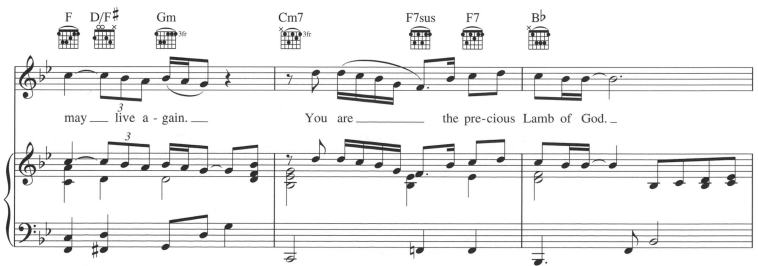

may ___ live a-gain. ___ You are ___ the pre-cious Lamb of God. ___

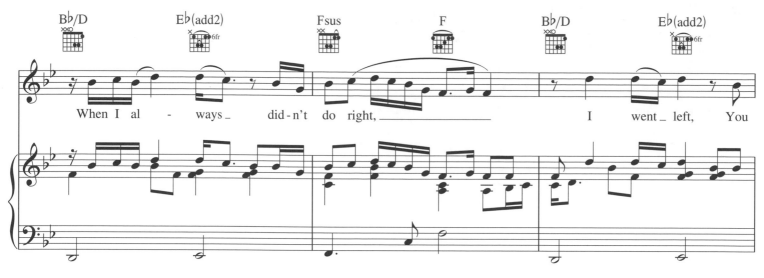

When I al - ways_ did-n't do right,_____ I went_ left, You

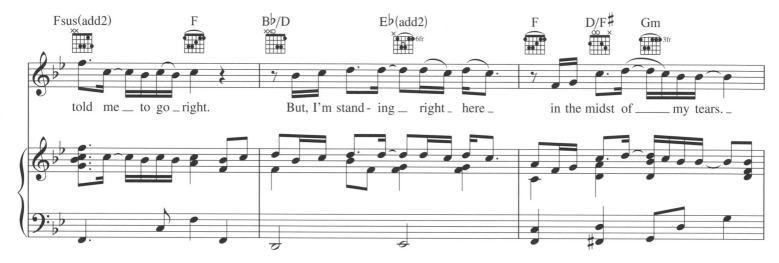

told me _ to go _ right._____ But, I'm stand - ing _ right _ here _ in the midst of _____ my tears. _

You are _____ the pre-cious Lamb of God. _ Thank You for _ the Lamb, _

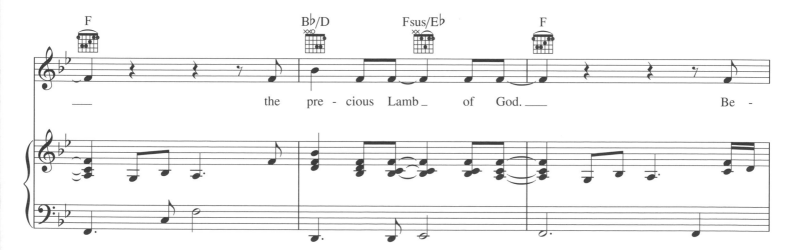

___ the pre - cious Lamb _ of God. ____ Be -

cause of Your grace _ I can fin - ish this race, _ the pre-cious Lamb _ of God. _

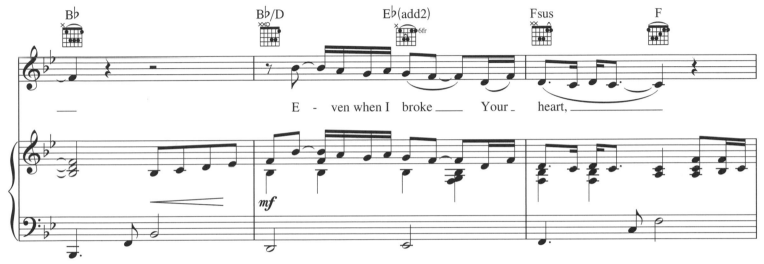

_ E - ven when I broke _ Your _ heart, _

mf

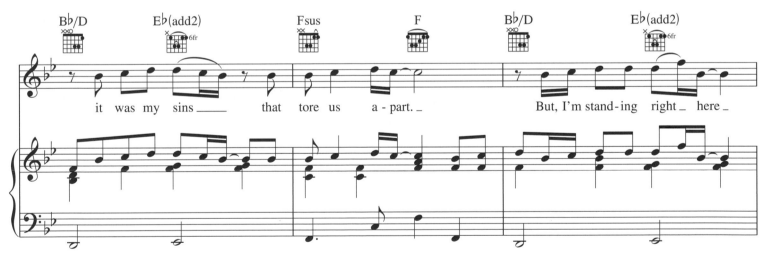

it was my sins _ that tore us a - part. _ But, I'm stand-ing right _ here _

in the midst of _ my tears. _ I claim You to be the Lamb of God. _

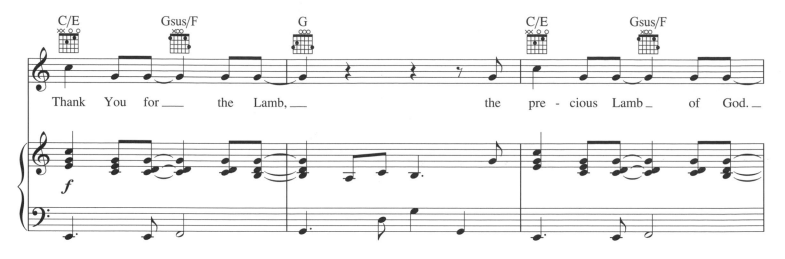

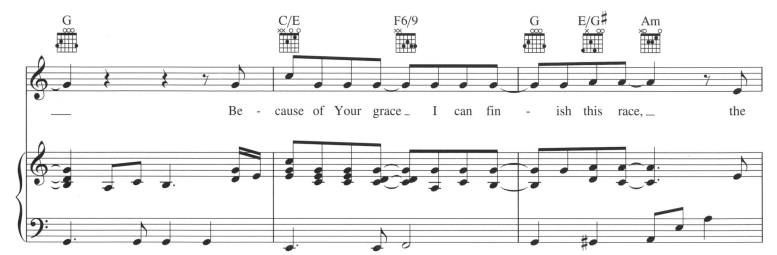

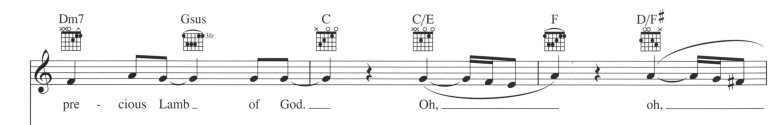

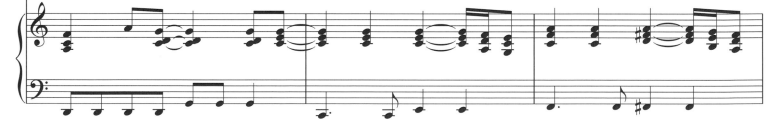

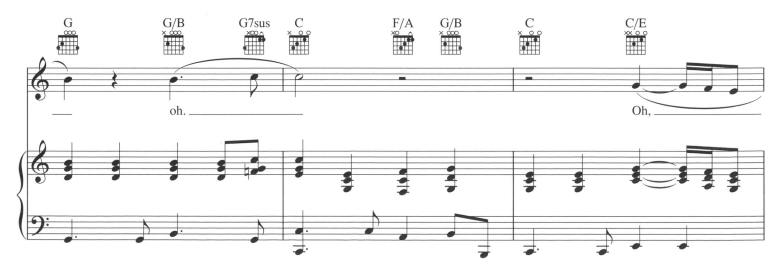

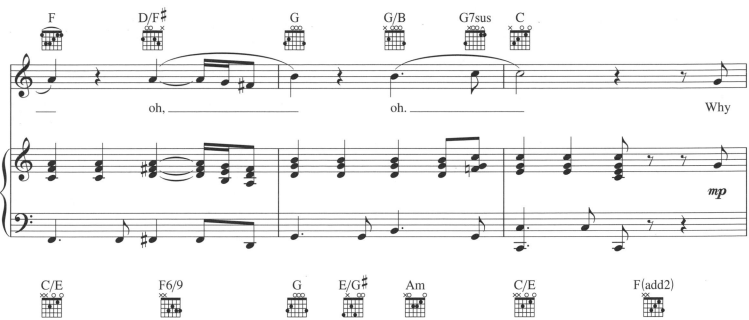

oh, _____ oh. _____ Why

You loved me so, ___ Lord, I shall ___ nev - er know. _

Why You loved me so, ___ Lord, I shall ___ nev - er know, _ the

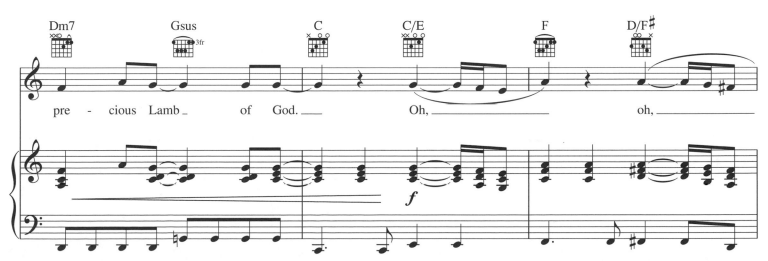

pre - cious Lamb _ of God. ___ Oh, _____ oh, _____

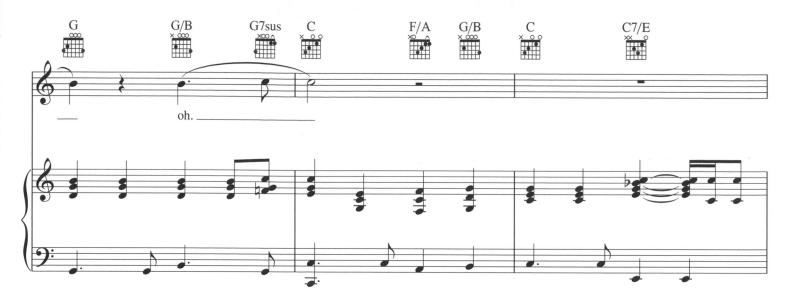

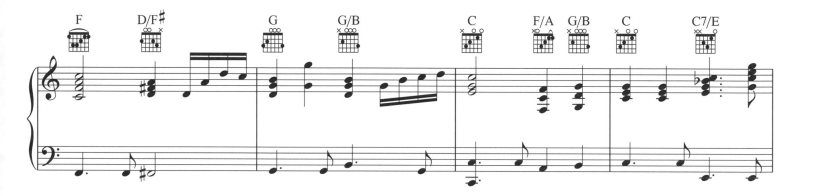

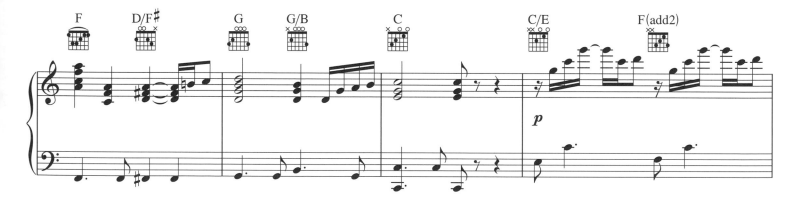

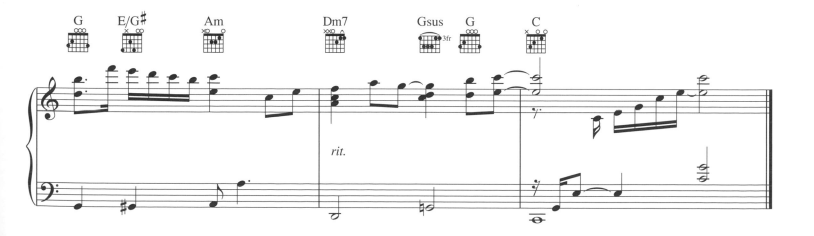

LOVE SOMEBODY

Words and Music by TOBY McKEEHAN,
AARON RICE, JAMIE MOORE,
CARY BARLOWE and MANDISA

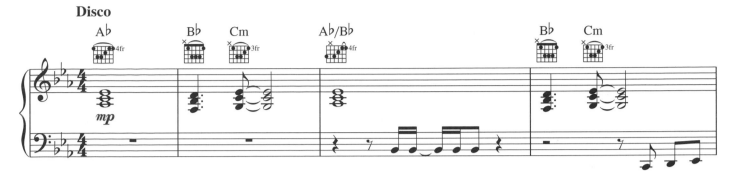

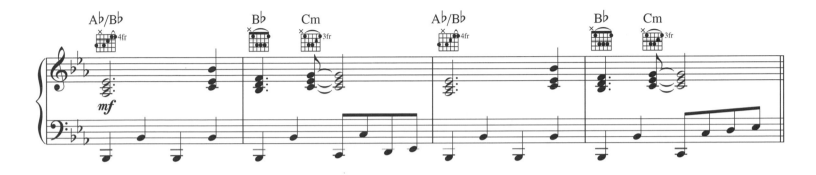

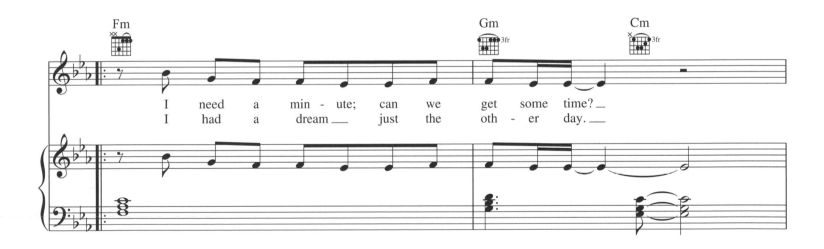

I need a min-ute; can we get some time? __
I had a dream __ can just the oth-er day. __

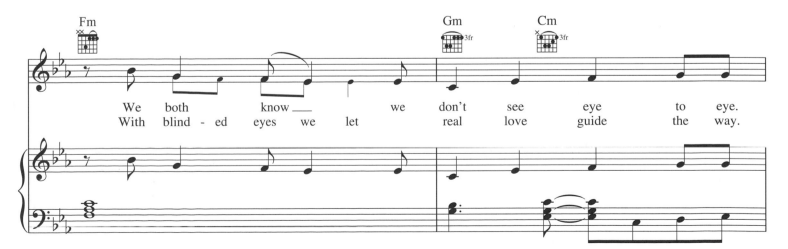

We both know __ we don't see eye to eye.
With blind-ed eyes we let real love guide the way.

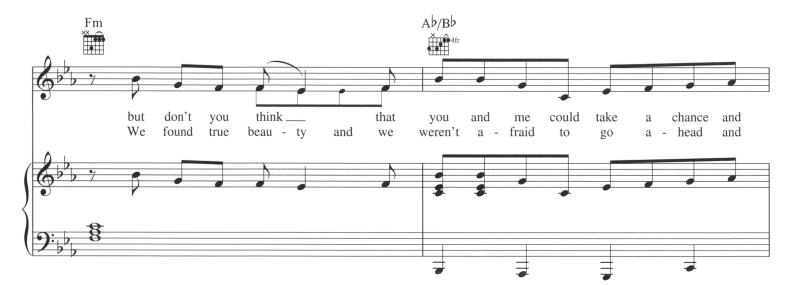

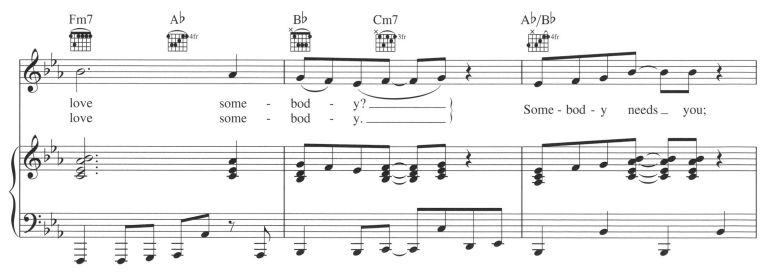

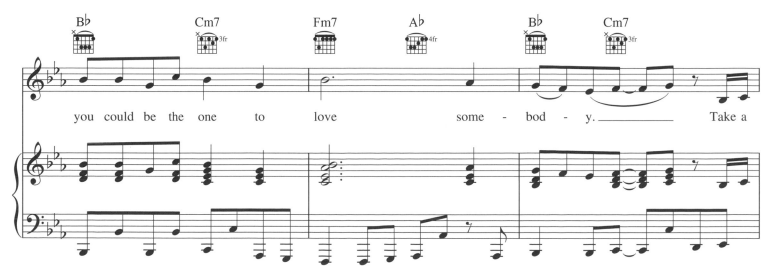

PRAISE HIM IN ADVANCE

Words and Music by
DEON KIPPING

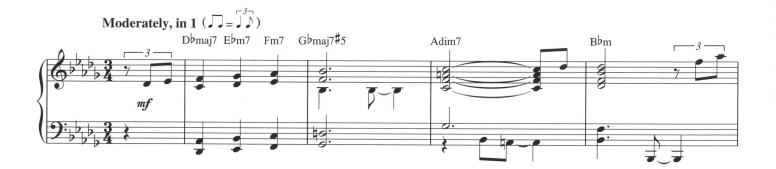

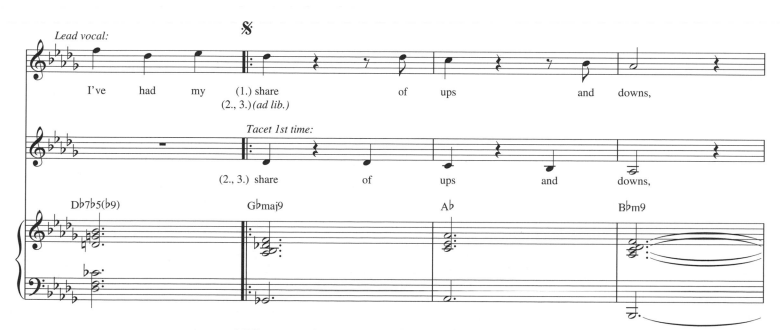

Lead vocal:

I've had my (1.) share of ups and downs,
(2., 3.)(ad lib.)

Tacet 1st time:

(2., 3.) share of ups and downs,

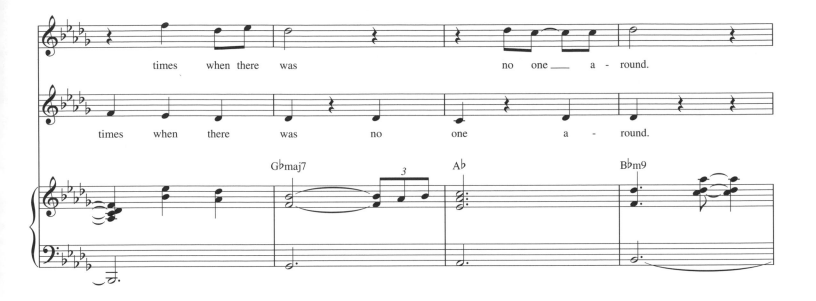

but I knew God would take them a-

way.

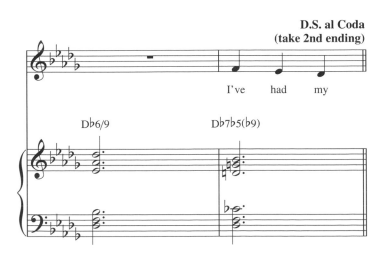

D.S. al Coda
(take 2nd ending)

I've had my

CODA

way. That's why I

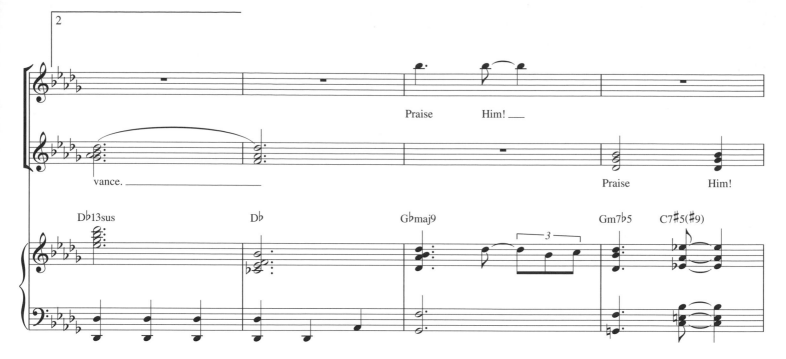

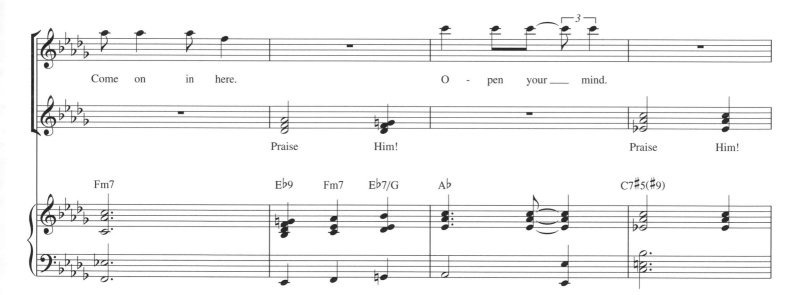

praise, come on ___ and praise Him.

Praise Him! Praise Him in ad-

Fm9   B♭m   Adim7   D♭/A♭   Gm7♭5   E♭9   A♭7

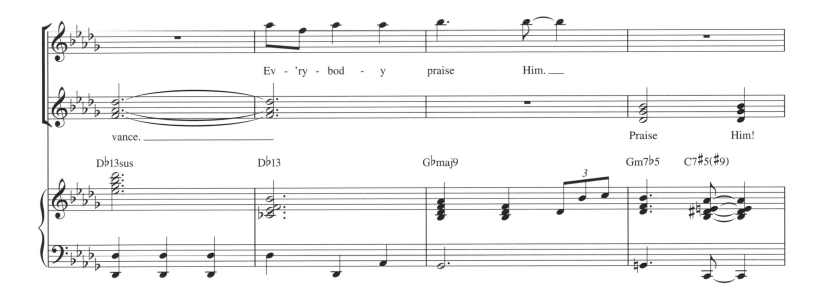

Ev - 'ry - bod - y praise Him. ___

vance. ___

Praise Him!

D♭13sus   D♭13   G♭maj9   Gm7♭5   C7♯5(♯9)

O - pen your mouth, give Him glo - ry,

Praise Him! Praise Him!

Fm7   E♭7   Fm7   Gm7♭5   A♭7   C7♯5(♯9)

straight eighths   *swing eighths*

tell your sto - ry.   Bless His name. __

Praise Him!   Praise Him!

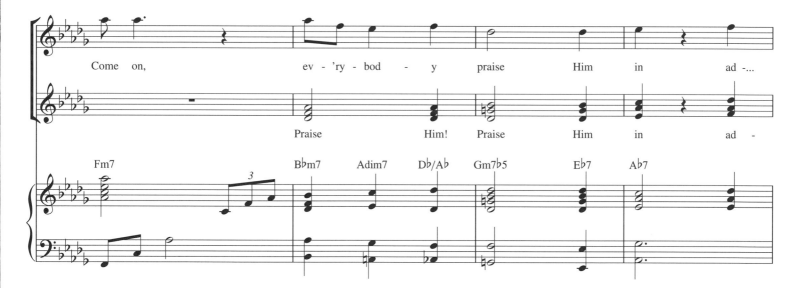

Come on,   ev-'ry-bod - y praise Him in ad -...

Praise Him! Praise Him in ad -

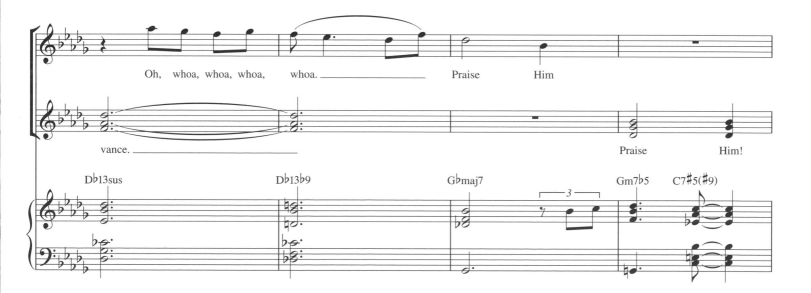

Oh, whoa, whoa, whoa,   whoa. ___ Praise Him

vance. ___   Praise Him!

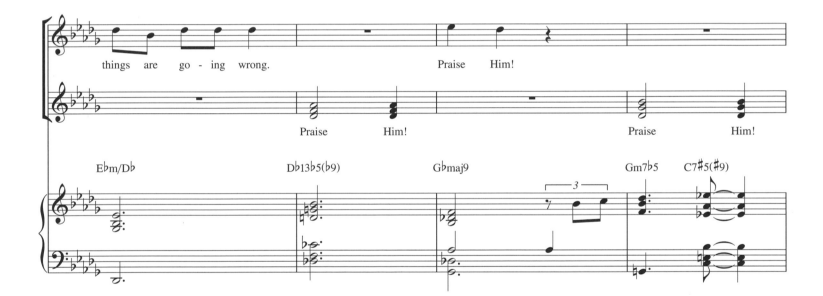

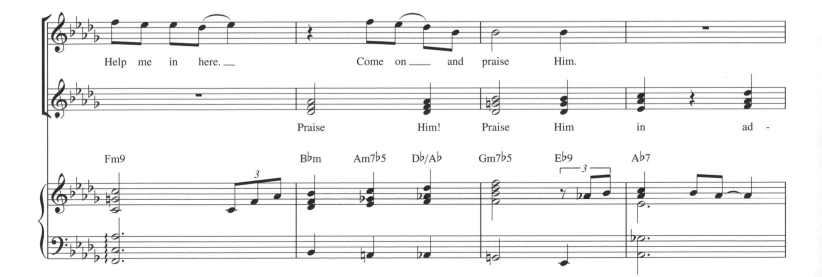

182

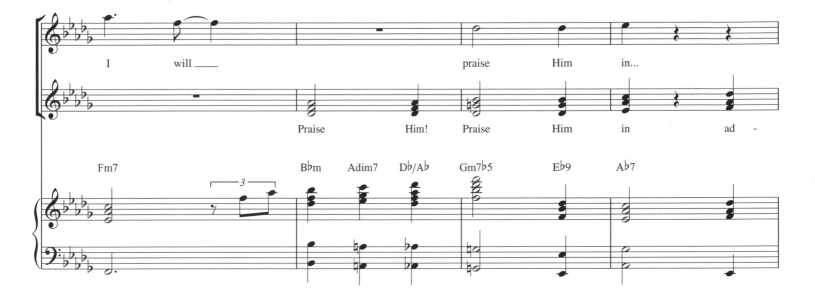

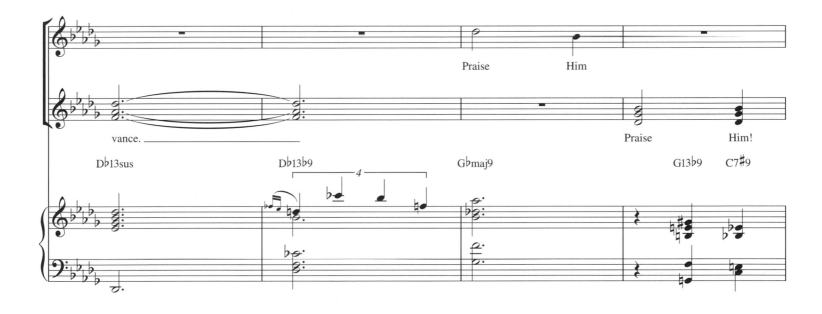

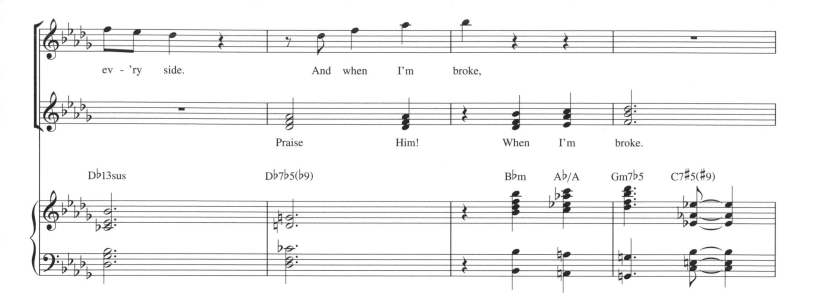

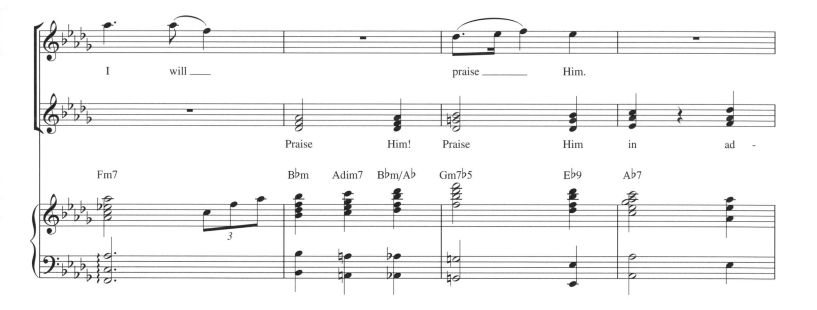

Whoa,   whoa.   (Whoa,   whoa.)   Whoa,   whoa.   (Whoa,   whoa.)

E♭m9   D♭maj13   C♭maj9   B♭m11

Whoa,   whoa.   (Whoa,   whoa.)   Whoa.

A♭m7   D♭13♭5(♭9)   D♭13   G♭maj9   A♭maj9

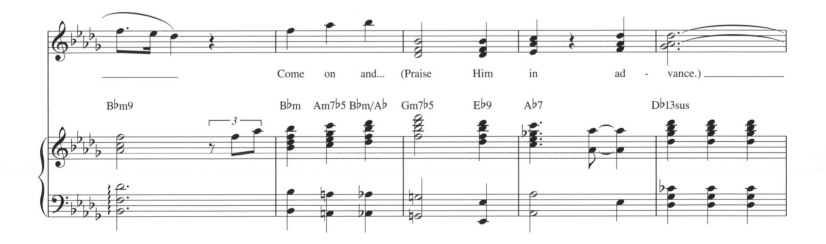

Come on and... (Praise Him in ad - vance.)

B♭m9   B♭m   Am7♭5   B♭m/A♭   Gm7♭5   E♭9   A♭7   D♭13sus

Whoa,   whoa.   (Whoa,   whoa.)   Whoa,   whoa.

D♭7   G♭maj9   D♭/F   E♭m11

SLIPPIN'

Words and Music by CECE WINANS,
SYLVIA BENNETT SMITH and DECONZO SMITH

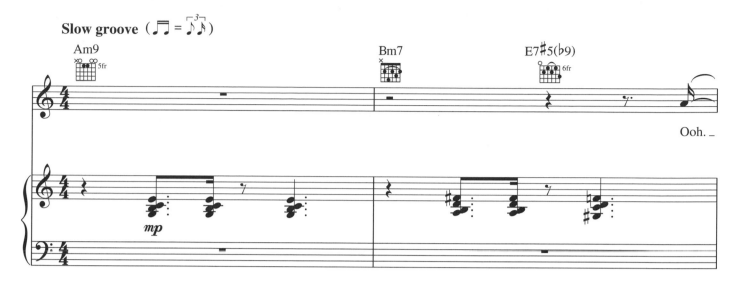

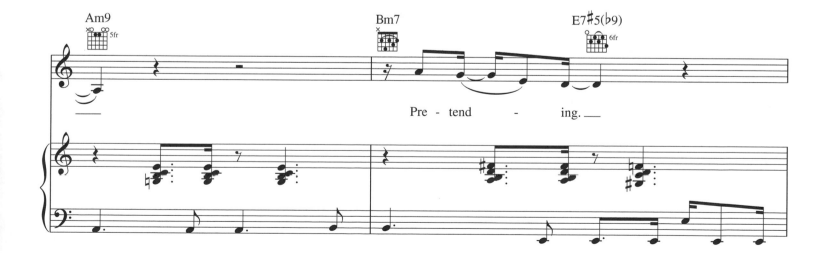

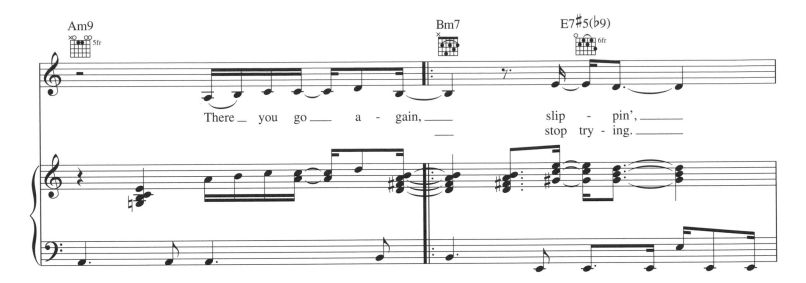

There__ you go__ a - gain,____ slip - pin',_____
stop try - ing.____

do - in' that thing__ you said__ you'd nev - er do a - gain.__
I've got the pow - er to keep__ you_____ from fall - ing.____

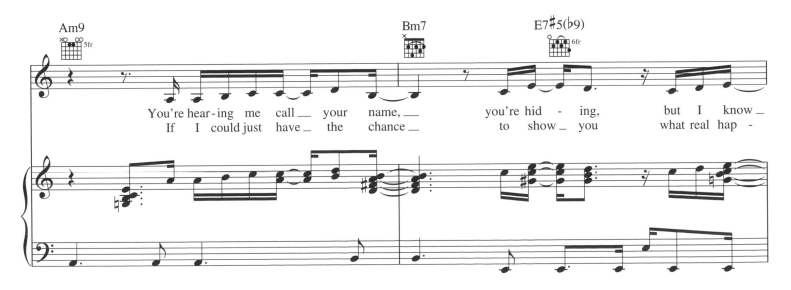

You're hear - ing me call__ your name,__ you're hid - ing, but I know__
If I could just have__ the chance__ to show__ you what real hap -

-na stay __ with me, ___ I need hon - es - ty. ___ Don't play with me, you're slip-

-pin'. _____ Can't __ make it on __ your own; __ -es - ty. ___ Don't play with me, you're slip -
Pre -

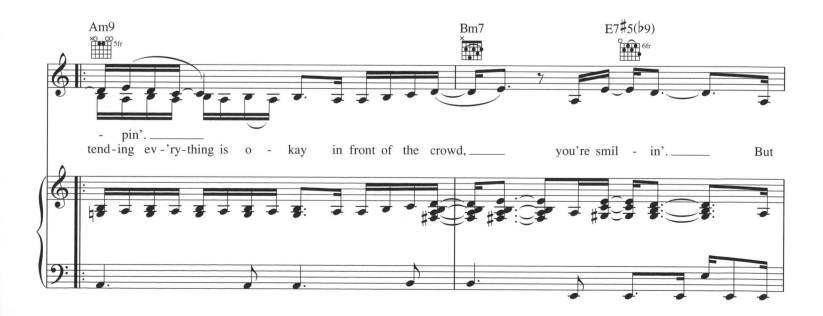

- pin'. _____ tend-ing ev - 'ry-thing is o - kay in front of the crowd, _____ you're smil - in'. _____ But

SO GOOD

Words and Music by MELINDA WATTS
and FREDDY WASHINGTON

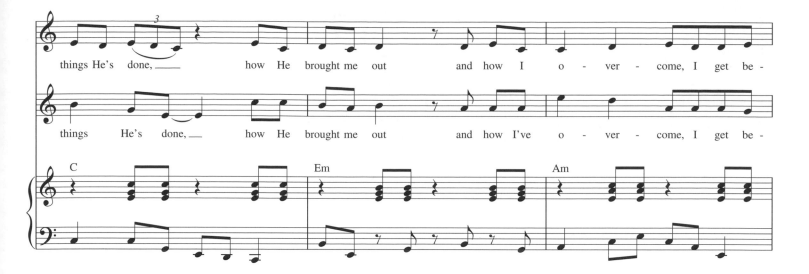

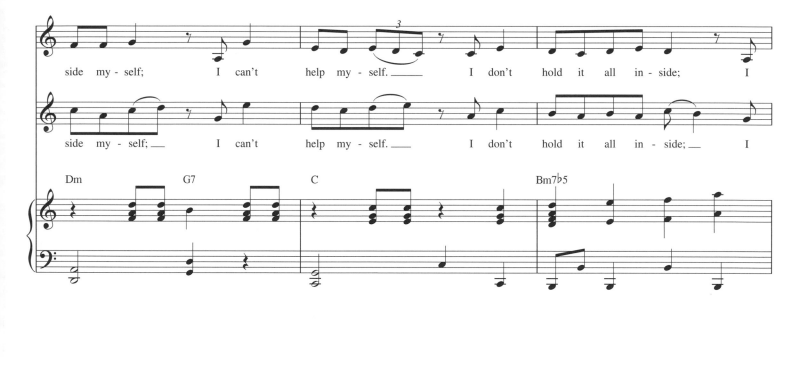

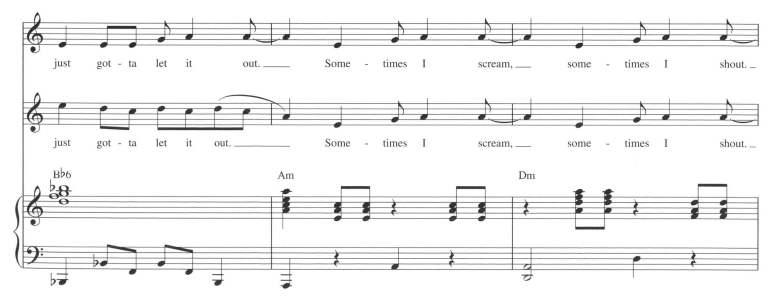

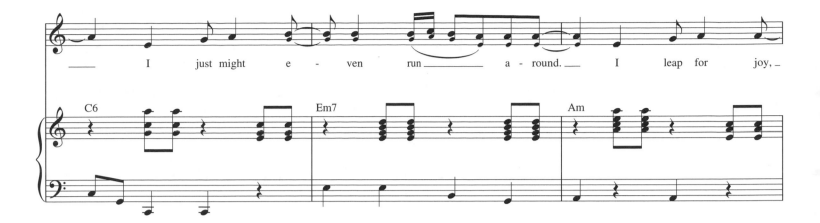

I just might e - ven run a - round. I leap for joy,

I lift my voice be - cause He's been so good to me.

Been so good to me. Been so...

Been so good to me. Been so,

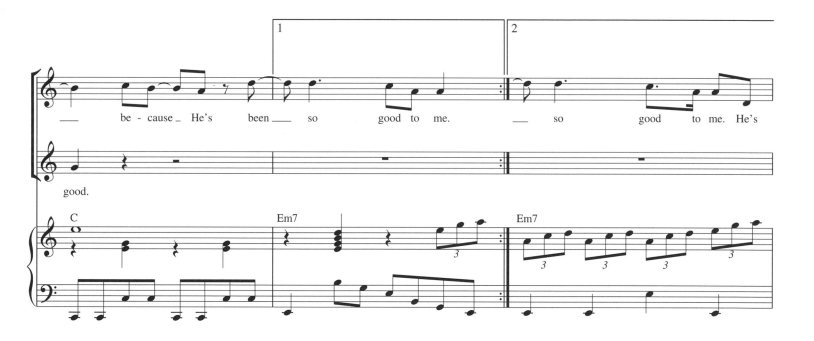

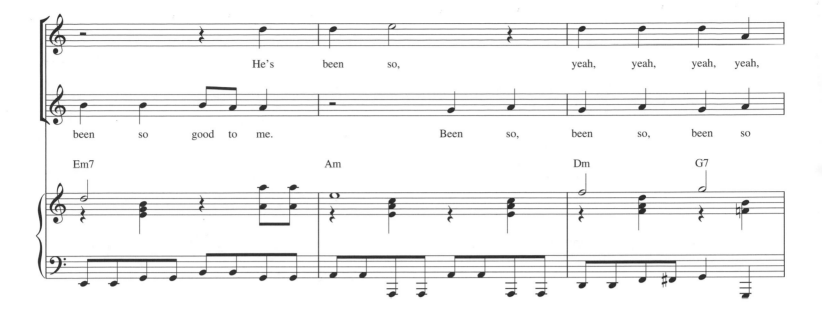

He's been so, yeah, yeah, yeah, yeah,

been so good to me. Been so, been so, been so

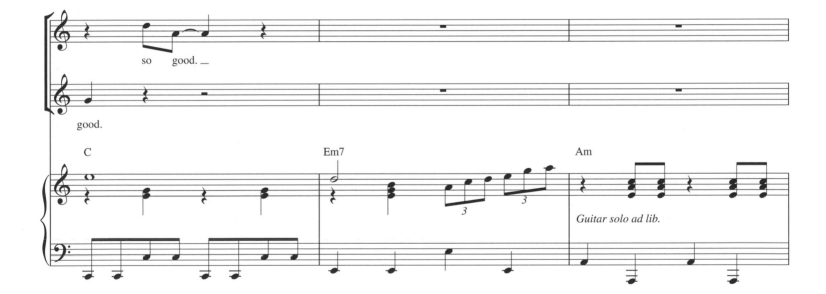

so good. ___

good.

Guitar solo ad lib.

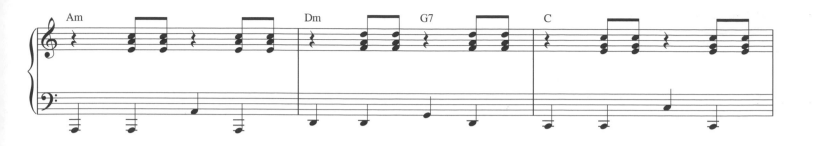

Been so good to me.

Been so good to me.

Been so good to me. Been so

Been so good to me. Been so

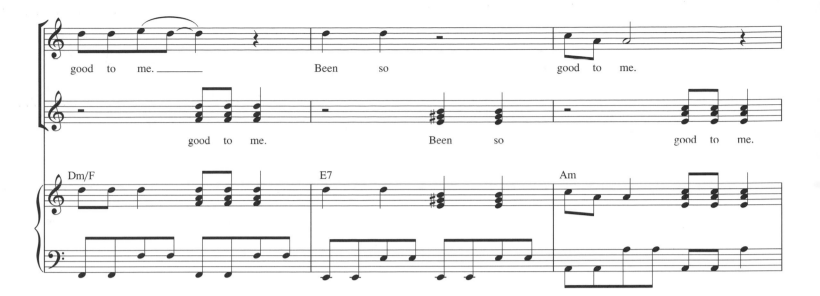

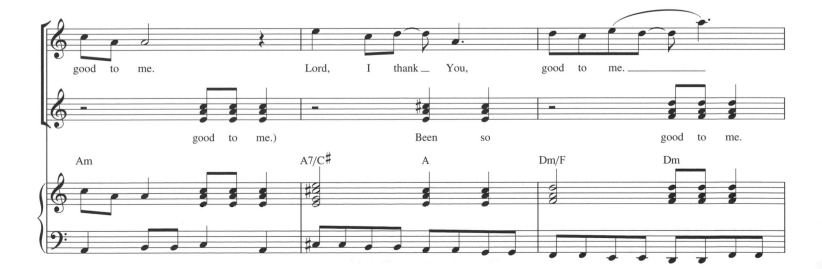

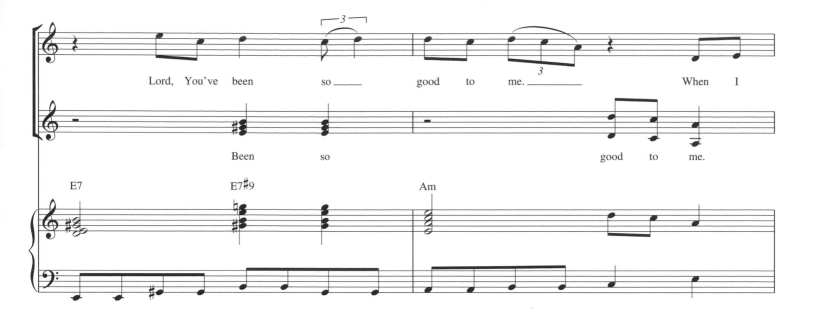

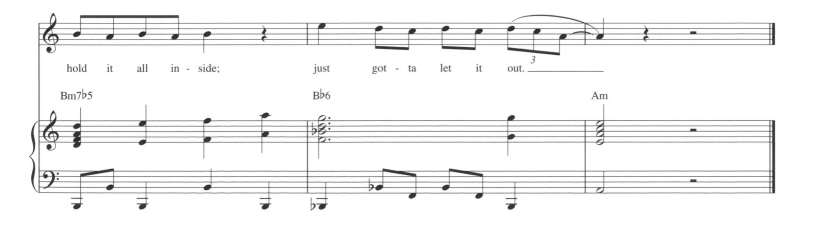

STAND

Words and Music by
DONNIE McCLURKIN

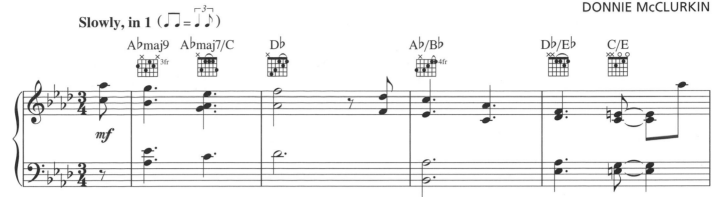

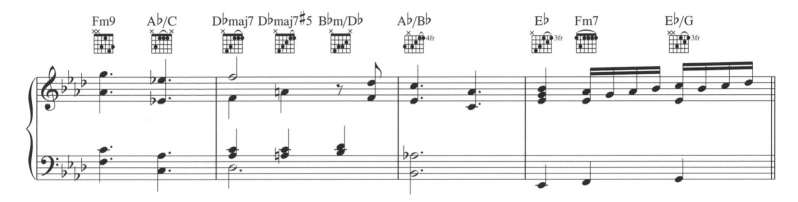

What do you do when you've done all you can___ and

it seems like___ it's nev - er___ e - nough? And_____

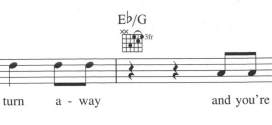

what do you say ____ when your ____ friends turn a - way and you're

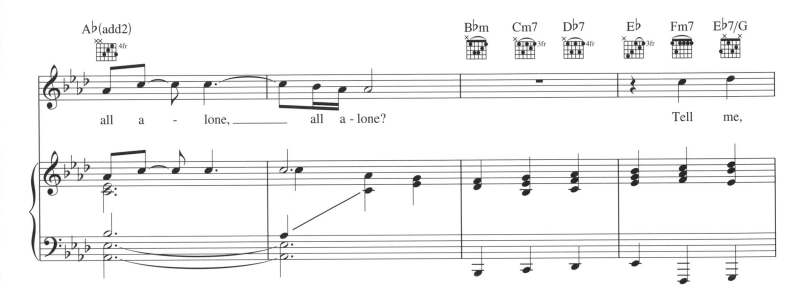

all a - lone, ____ all a - lone? Tell me,

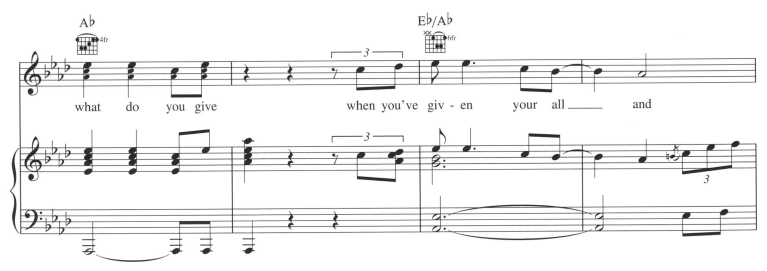

what do you give when you've giv - en your all ____ and

seems like ____ you can't make ____ it ____ through? Well, you just

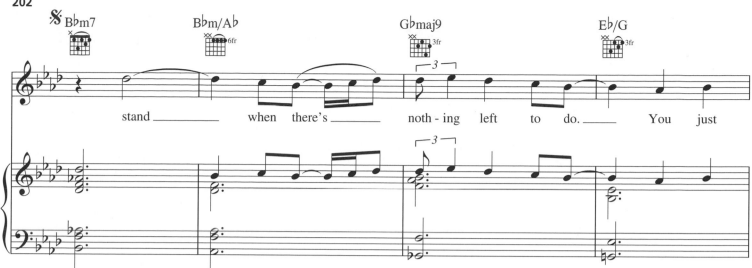

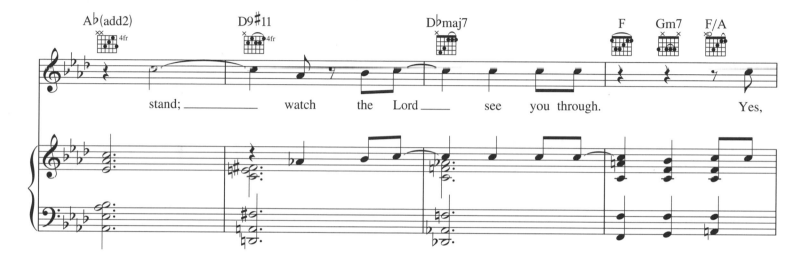

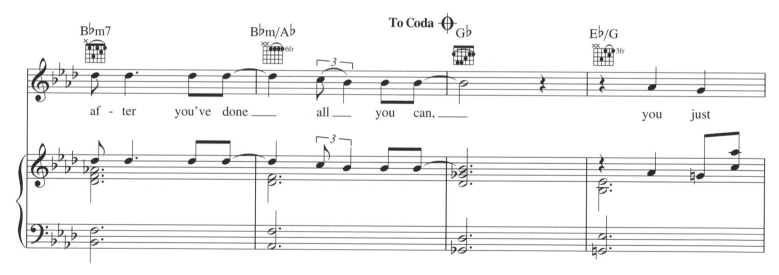

how do you han - dle the guilt of ___ your past?

Tell me, how _____ do you deal ___ with the shame? And _____

how can you smile ___ while your _____ heart has been bro - ken and ___

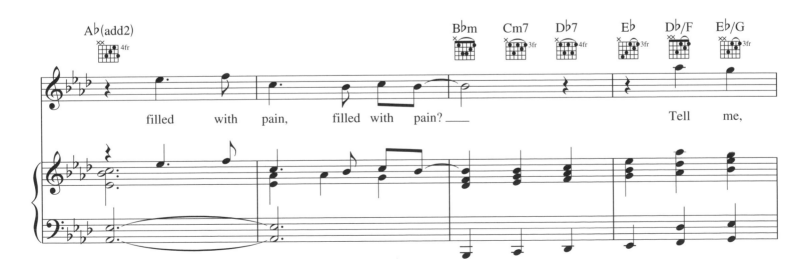

filled with pain, filled with pain? ___ Tell me,

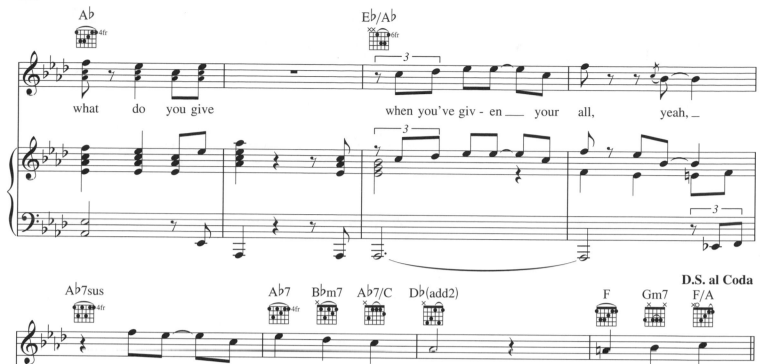

what do you give   when you've giv-en ___ your all, yeah, ___

D.S. al Coda

seems like ___ you can't make it through?   Child, you just

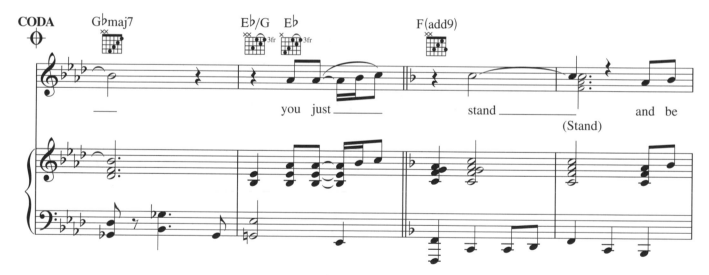

CODA

you just ___ stand ___ and be
(Stand)

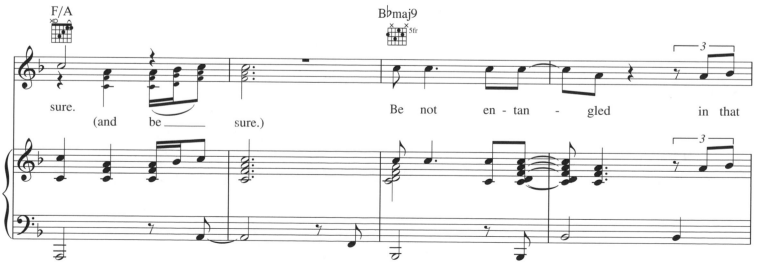

sure.
(and be ___ sure.)   Be not en-tan-gled   in that

WHO IS LIKE THE LORD

Words and Music by
ISRAEL HOUGHTON

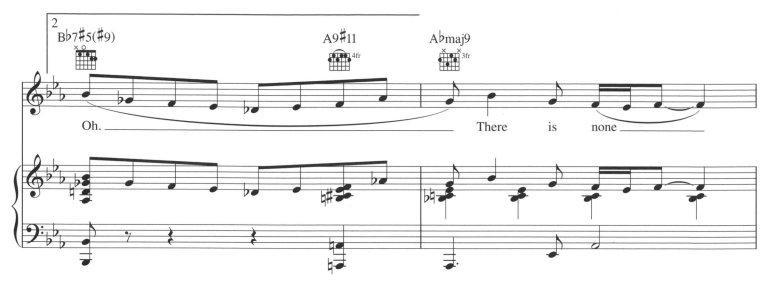

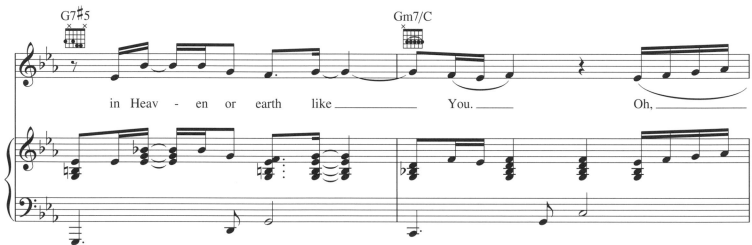

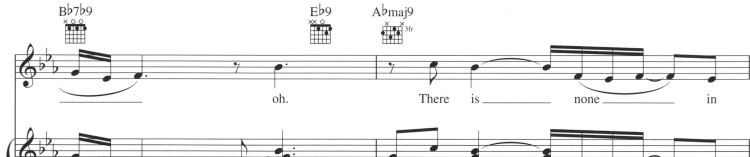

216

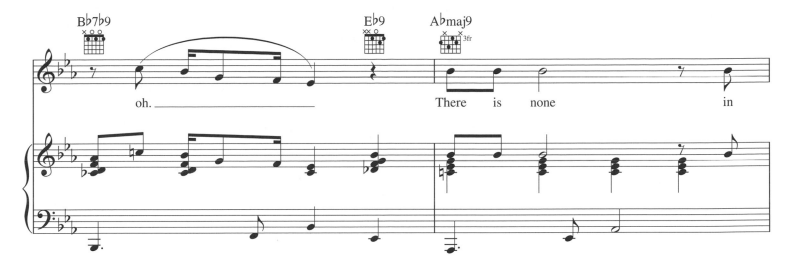

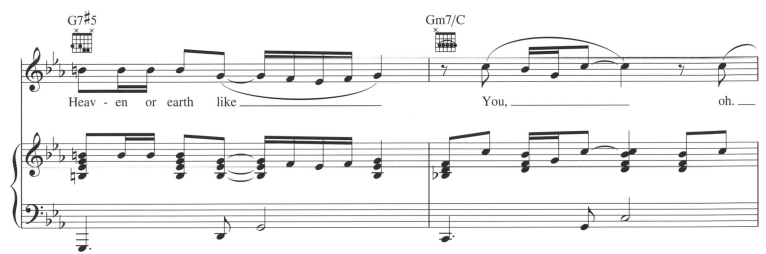

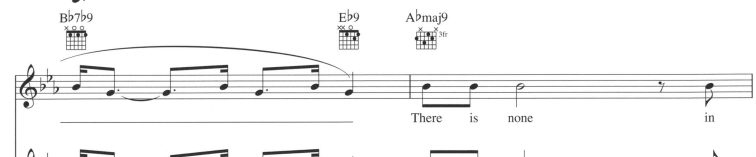

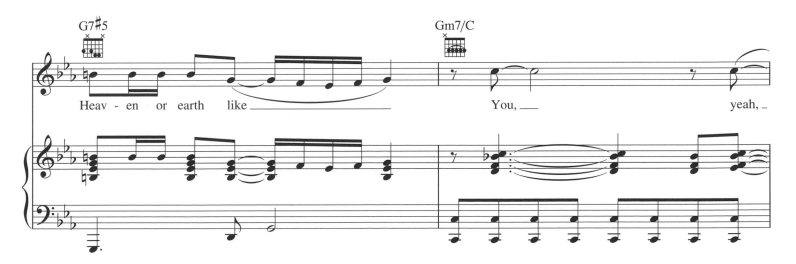

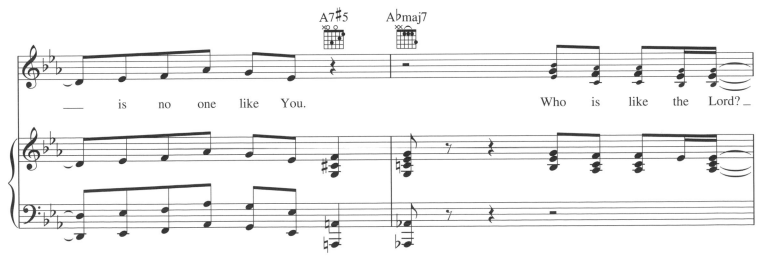

STRENGTH

Words and Music by
JOHN P. KEE

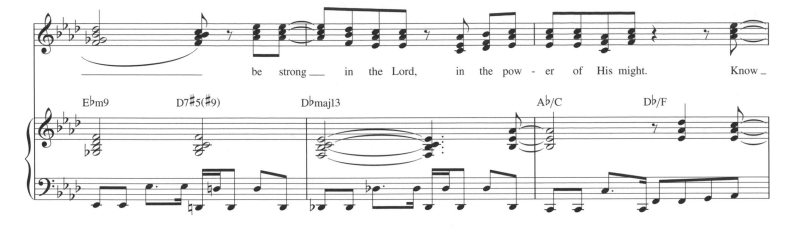

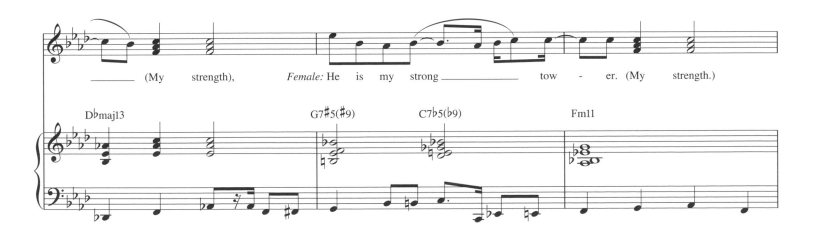

Male:
Strength to know You're com - ing soon, _ (my strength). *Female:* I know Your strength can be re-newed.

Be strong, yeah, be strong. I was strength-ened in my
(Lead vocals ad lib.)

spir - it when He spoke to __ me. No more fear; I have peace.

Who the Son sets free, I know real - ly is free in - deed. Oh, ___

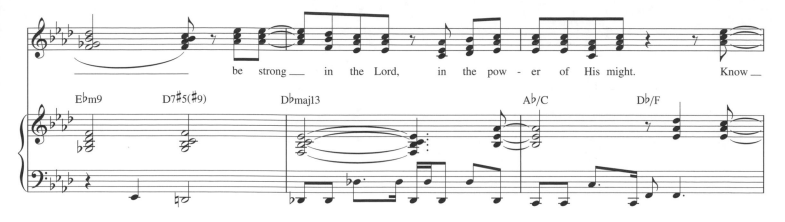

be strong ___ in the Lord, in the pow - er of His might. Know ___

___ in your heart, ev - 'ry bat - tle He will fight. Oh. ___

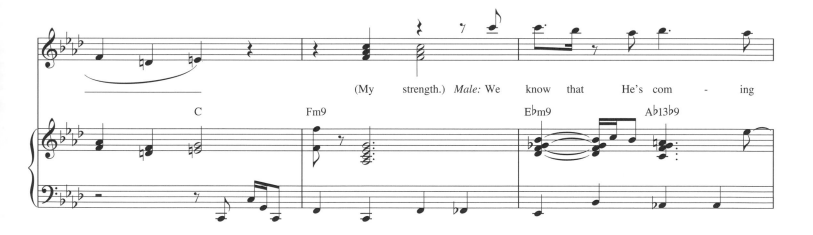

(My strength.) *Male:* We know that He's com - ing

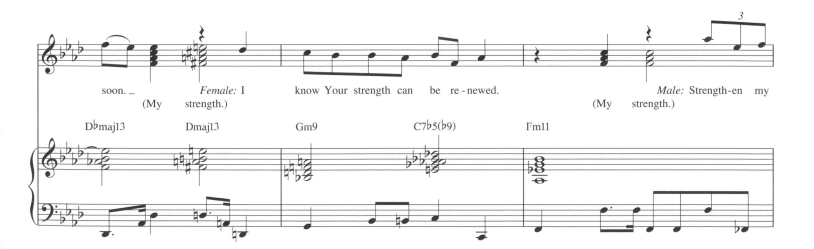

soon. _ *Female:* I know Your strength can be re - newed. *Male:* Strength-en my
(My strength.) (My strength.)

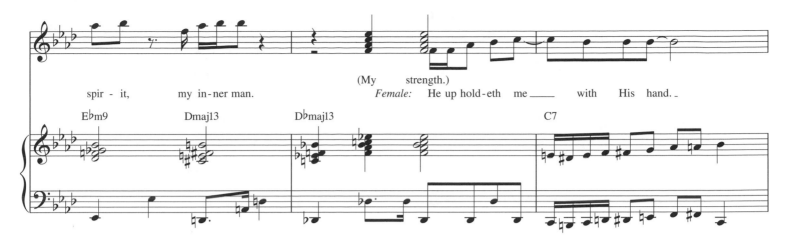

(My strength.)

spir - it, my in-ner man. *Female:* He up hold-eth me ___ with His hand. _

Ebm9   Dmaj13   Dbmaj13   C7

Oh. ___   Oh. ___

Fm   C   Fm

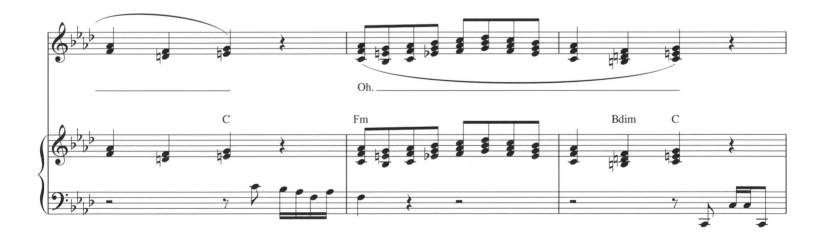

___   Oh. ___

C   Fm   Bdim   C

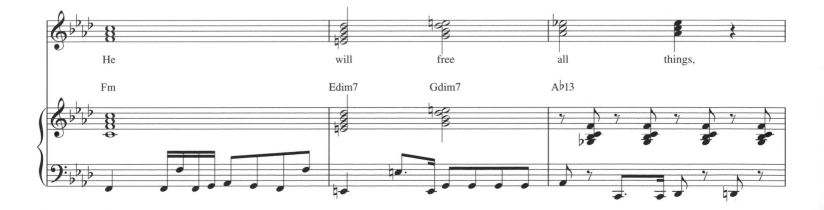

He   will   free   all   things,

Fm   Edim7   Gdim7   Ab13

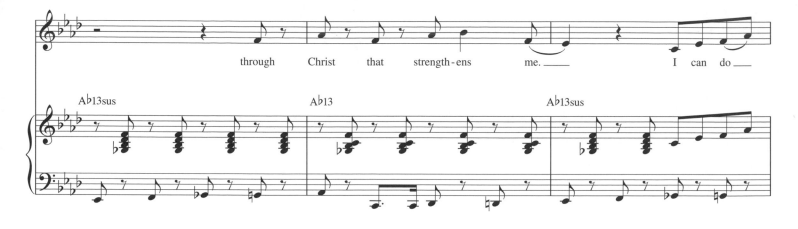

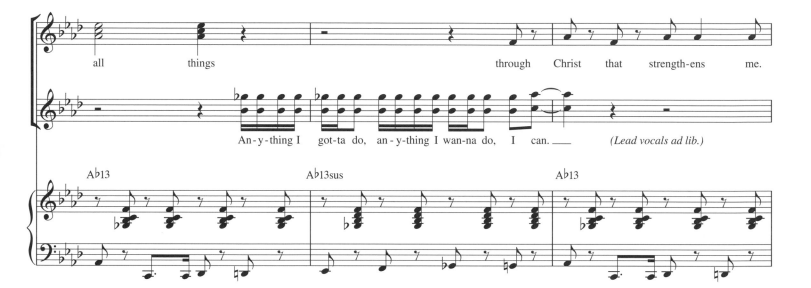

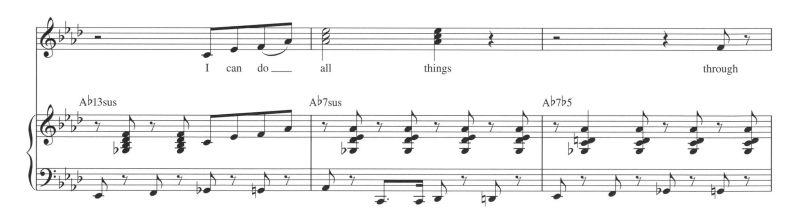

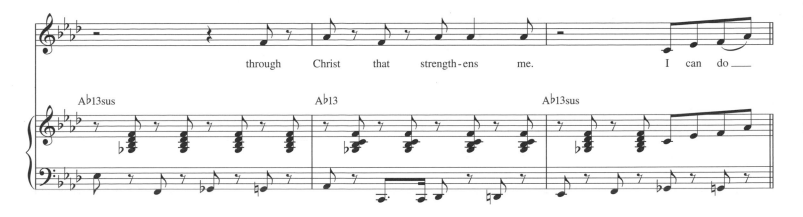

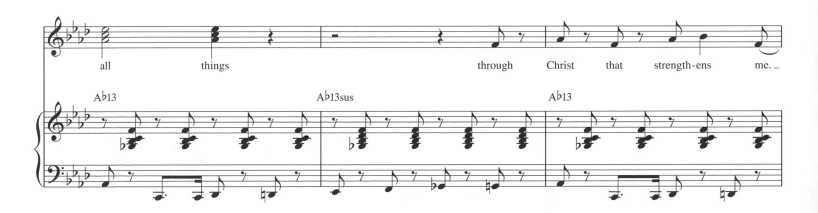

WHERE LOVE BEGINS

Words and Music by GORDON CHAMBERS,
DENISE RICH, TROY TAYLOR
and RICHARD WILLIAMS

Moderately

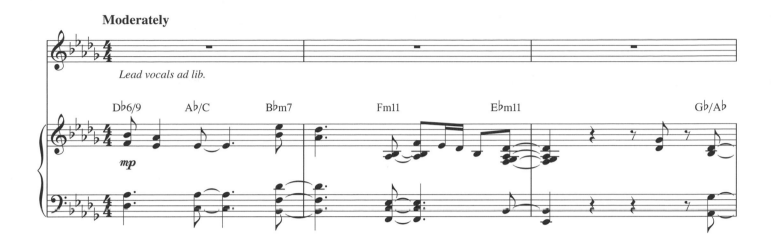

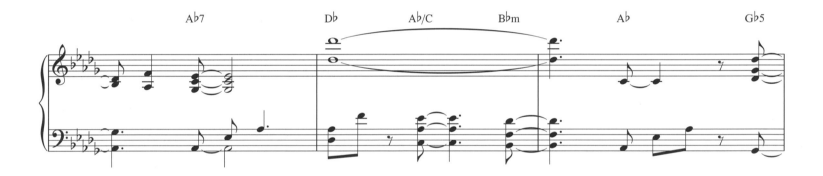

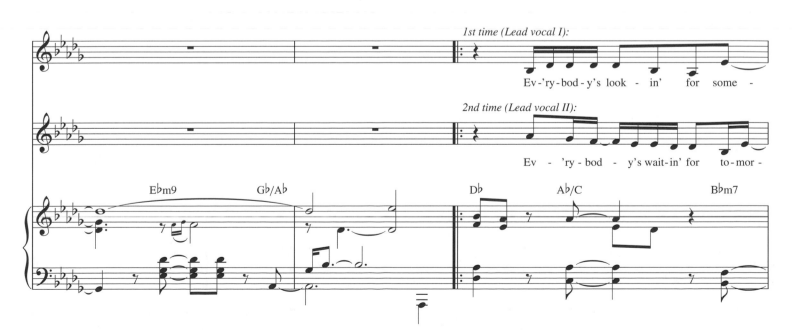

1st time (Lead vocal I):

Ev-'ry-bod-y's look-in' for some-

2nd time (Lead vocal II):

Ev-'ry-bod-y's wait-in' for to-mor-

- thing, _____ an an-swer to be-lieve in. _____

- row _____ to do what they could do to-day. _____

A♭   G♭5   E♭m9   A♭7sus   A♭

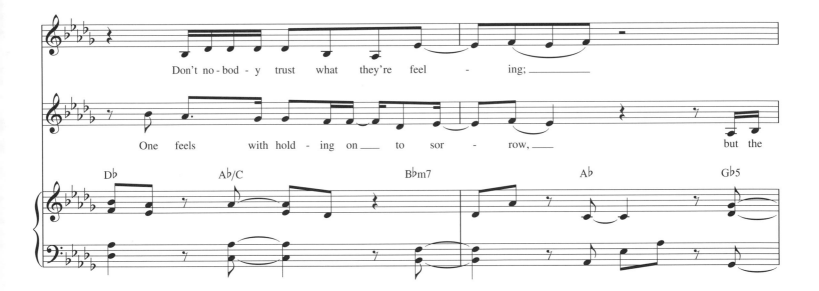

Don't no-bod-y trust what they're feel - ing; _____

One feels with hold-ing on ___ to sor - row, _____ but the

D♭   A♭/C   B♭m7   A♭   G♭5

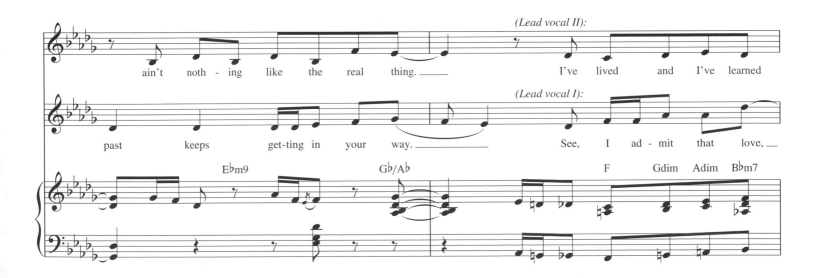

(Lead vocal II):

ain't noth-ing like the real thing. _____ I've lived and I've learned

past keeps get-ting in your way. _____

(Lead vocal I):

See, I ad-mit that love, ___

E♭m9   G♭/A♭   F Gdim Adim B♭m7

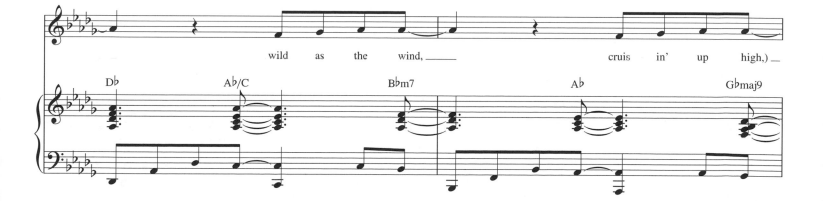

and I've got faith on my wings. (There's no look-ing back.

You've for-giv-en my sins. The truth is my song,)

and it comes deep from with-in, (be-cause that's where love be-gins.)

(Lead vocals ad lib.)

The voice in my heart won't leave ___ me a - lone. ___

(-lone, ___

F Gdim F/A B♭m   A♭m7   D♭7   G♭maj7

That's why I'll keep on, ___ keep on ___ hold - ing

no.) ___

Fm7   E♭m11   G♭/A♭

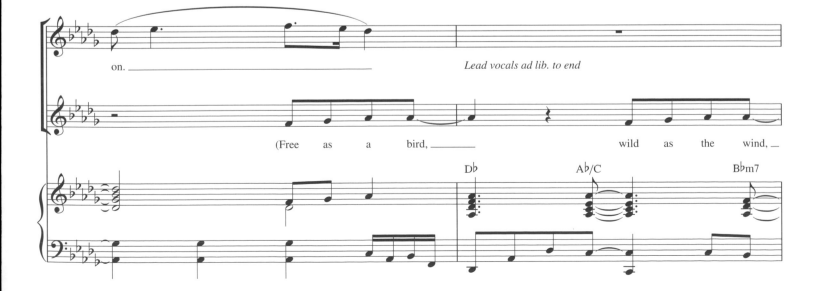

on. ___   *Lead vocals ad lib. to end*

(Free as a bird, ___   wild as the wind, __

D♭   A♭/C   B♭m7

238

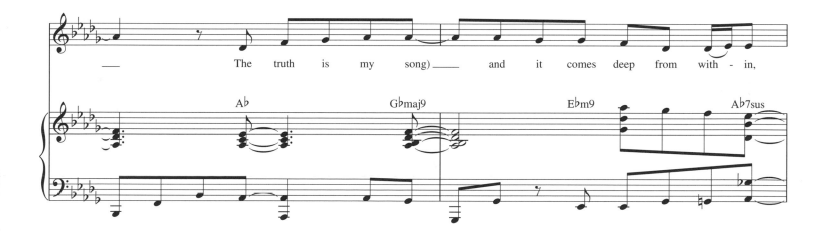

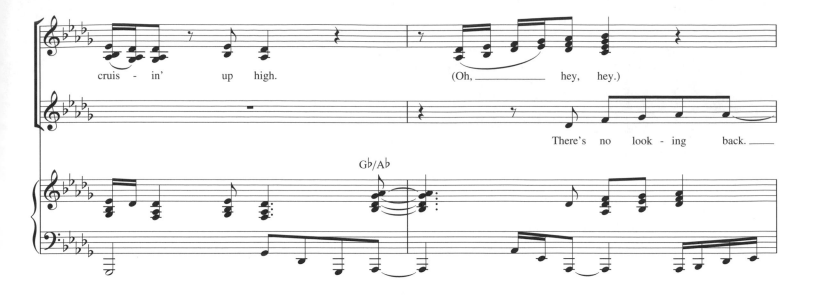

cruis - in' up high. (Oh, _____ hey, hey.)

There's no look - ing back. _____

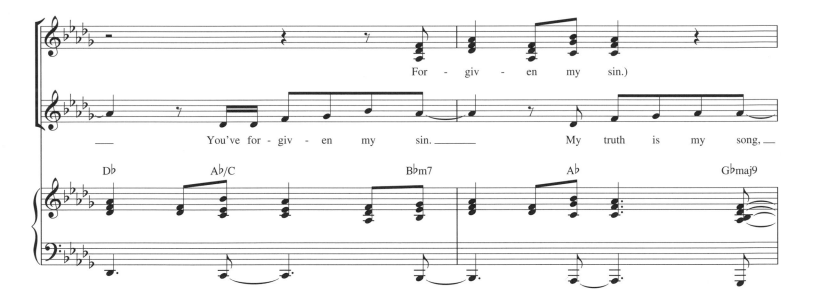

For - giv - en my sin.)

_____ You've for - giv - en my sin. _____ My truth is my song, _____

_____ be - cause that's where love be - gins.) _____

More Contemporary Christian Folios from

Arranged for Piano, Voice and Guitar

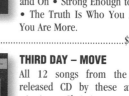